nine
days of
eternity

ANKE EVERTZ

nine
days of
eternity

An extraordinary
near-death experience that
teaches us about life and beyond

HAY HOUSE

Carlsbad, California • New York City
London • Sydney • New Delhi

Published in the United Kingdom by:
Hay House UK Ltd, The Sixth Floor, Watson House
54 Baker Street, London W1U 7BU
Tel: +44 (0)20 3927 7290; Fax: +44 (0)20 3927 7291
www.hayhouse.co.uk

Published in the United States of America by:
Hay House Inc., PO Box 5100, Carlsbad, CA 92018-5100
Tel: (1) 760 431 7695 or (800) 654 5126
Fax: (1) 760 431 6948 or (800) 650 5115; www.hayhouse.com

Published in Australia by:
Hay House Australia Ltd, 18/36 Ralph St, Alexandria NSW 2015
Tel: (61) 2 9669 4299; Fax: (61) 2 9669 4144; www.hayhouse.com.au

Published in India by:
Hay House Publishers India, Muskaan Complex,
Plot No.3, B-2, Vasant Kunj, New Delhi 110 070
Tel: (91) 11 4176 1620; Fax: (91) 11 4176 1630; www.hayhouse.co.in

A catalogue record for this book is available from the British Library.

Tradepaper ISBN: 978-1-4019-7347-6
E-book ISBN: 978-1-78817-958-4
Audiobook ISBN: 978-1-78817-959-1

10 9 8 7 6 5 4 3 2 1

Printed in the United States of America

Interior images: www.shutterstock.com

You Miracle

You two-legged miracle...
You miracle with your mighty spirit.
You miracle of conscious Creation.
You must remember!

You two-legged miracle...
You miracle with your abundant creativity.
Did you know that you have the power
to choose in every moment?

You two-legged miracle...
You miracle with your limitless power.
Are you using the power of your mind?
To what do you give your attention?

Stop pretending to be helpless!
Stop pretending to be powerless!
Stop pretending to be small,
dependent, bound, incapable!

You miracle with your limitless creative power.
Wake up from your dream and remember!

That's why you're here.

Contents

Preface

My story began one autumn evening more than a decade ago when my clothing accidently caught alight as I stood by the fireplace in my living room. Before long, my entire body was on fire, and it dawned on me that I was about to die. But this realization didn't trigger panic or fear in me; instead, I felt a deep sense of peace and serenity. Even as my lungs gasped desperately for air, the stress just melted away and I found myself thinking that whatever came my way, I was ready for it.

Even today, I can't fully explain what happened next, but I know that it marked the beginning of the most miraculous and enlightening experience of my life. Suddenly, I was ejected from my burning body and found myself observing it from the *outside*. A feeling of neutral detachment came over me and from that pivotal moment on, there were two of me, and I felt barely any connection to my physical body.

I watched the doctors' efforts to save my life and saw them put me into a drug-induced coma. My severely burned body struggled to survive for nine days, and my friends and family feared the worst, but all that time, I was feeling more alive than ever before. In my limitless, bodiless state, I was taking an incredible journey, traveling beyond space and time, beyond human imagination, visiting realms of consciousness and Creation I'd never imagined existed.

I couldn't have known it at the time, but it's clear to me now that I walked through the fire that evening – in the real sense of the saying – only to return nine days later an entirely new person.

The Greatest Gift

Today, when people ask me who I am, I find it very difficult to answer in a few short sentences. I'd love to reply, all bright-eyed and earnest, 'I'm everything,' but I rarely do. More often, I'll say, rather cautiously: 'I'm a person with two lives: a life before death and a life after death.'

I find it almost impossible to reminisce about the life I led before my accident because for some reason I can remember little about it. However, I *do* recall that the old me was stuck in a rut and felt worthless, unloved, and unbearably lonely. I'd no idea what made me happy, what fulfilled me, and I had to fight a constant urge to 'get out' – out of my body, out of my feelings, and out of the life I found so incredibly difficult.

However, while my body lay in a coma for nine days, a nameless teacher invited me to consciously explore my bigger, more complete, and wiser self – my True Self. I received extensive training about the real meaning of my life and the relationships that were part of it, diving deep into the heart of Creation to find it again within every cell in my body.

Prompted by this new and radically improved view of myself, I consciously decided to return to my body and live my life a second time, and every day since then I've experienced it as a miracle. I feel truly at home in my body, as well as connected to my True Self, to whom I've given full control over the direction of my life.

All the values, ambitions, and motivations I had before the accident no longer make sense to me – instead, my life takes the shape of my inner fullness and joy. I've learned to let things come to me, to express what needs to be expressed, to let my emotions come and go, and to no longer stand in the way of this flow.

Our Common Journey

Do you believe in miracles? Do you feel safe in the knowledge that you're a part of an inexhaustible source of creativity and infinite possibilities? Do you feel, deep down, that your life has so much more to offer than what's been revealed to you so far? Do you know why you're here on Earth? I can tell you why you're *not* here. You're certainly not here to feel small and powerless. You're not here to pay off a debt, or as a punishment, or to pass a test. You're also not alone, or disconnected from everything you dream of, even if it may feel that way sometimes. No one's forgotten you, no one's judging you, no one expects anything from you. You're not here to climb the ladder of success or to be rewarded for your good deeds.

You're here to *remember* everything that's always been (and always will be) an inseparable part of you. You're here to recognize your limitless creative power and stop hiding from yourself. You're here to expand your consciousness into all possible realms, to enrich yourself and the world around you. I want to remind you of everything that you *really* are, to let in the bright light that's waiting to be discovered in every one of the 80 trillion cells of your body.

Although this book is about my personal journey, it's also about *your* journey because we come from the same Source. In this life we've sought out very similar challenges and experiences, and even though they may differ on one level or another, they have the same origin. We're all figuring out how we can master life's challenges and experiences, and we all want to find our way back to our true home.

How This Book Came About

It took me almost 10 years to share my story with more than just a handful of people; I was afraid of going public with the greatest, most personal experience of my life, of not being able to convey it in words that did justice to its magic and miracles. But after a lot of love and encouragement from my wonderful editor, I started to write this book.

I quickly realized that it was impossible for me to approach the task using only my head. Whenever I thought about my life before the fire or tried to find ways to describe in detail my near-death experience, I'd get a headache. The more I tried to explain everything I'd seen and heard during my coma from my perspective, the more blocked I felt.

However, there were also countless occasions when I'd wake in the middle of the night and sit down at my computer with a steaming cup of coffee, my fingers flying across the keyboard, filling page after page, without me ever feeling truly present. Most of the time, I felt more like a curious fellow-reader than the author of what I'd written.

But my reason for writing *Nine Days of Eternity* was clear from the start. I didn't just want to tell an exciting story that fed the mind with new explanations for something miraculous and inexplicable. I wanted to go deeper and touch the heart of the reader. My wish was that the book would form a bridge between our physical reality and our spiritual home. If I could, I'd take every single person on this beautiful Earth by the hand and *show* them – and above all make them *feel* – who they really are.

I know that's impossible, but I also know that this book will find its way to exactly the right people – those who are willing to look behind the walls they erect and the show they put on for others. Let me take *you* on a journey. I want to tell you who you really are. For it's my heart's desire that you, too, remember where you came from.

May this book support you as you expand your consciousness; may it take you into realms you've only ever imagined; and may it take you beyond anything you thought possible. It may well turn your current view of yourself and your life upside down and inside out. As you read on, you may question what I'm telling you, or even dismiss it as nonsense, but all I ask is that you try to understand the realities we'll explore together, and be aware that it's unimaginably difficult, if not impossible, to find the words to describe something so incomprehensible.

This book contains a treasure that should be discovered by every person who wants to live a fulfilled life – a life in which they're in tune with themselves. But it's not about the conventional idea of 'happiness' that so many people strive for. It goes deeper than that, taking you further into yourself than you may have gone before. Because we all have access to Creation, God, the Source – whatever we call it – and it wants to express itself through us.

All I ask is that you read my words and feel the vibration within. This book is *your* wake-up call. Are you ready to walk through the fire with me? Are you ready to rediscover your True Self?

PART I

The Turning Point in My Life

CHAPTER 1

Behind the Smokescreen

I was still relatively young when I realized that not everything in this life could or would go right. There was something wrong with the world into which I'd been born, but I couldn't explain why. I'd often hear a gentle, quiet voice inside me saying that I needed to wake up and see things as they really were.

As a child I'd watch the adults around me and marvel at the way they interacted; I couldn't understand why they were so hurtful to one other, why they always put their own needs first, why they always played power games. Shouting, fighting, and arguing were relationship behaviors that I witnessed but couldn't make any sense of.

In fact, little in life made sense to me. People seemed to change from one moment to the next, and everything I thought was true turned out to be the opposite. My young mind searched for explanations, but it just couldn't figure things out. Was what was happening in the world around me real? Or was the truth that I felt and sensed deep down inside me closer to reality? Was I living in a dream world? Was everything merely an illusion? But if it was, it was all so incredibly magical, realistic, tangible, and credible.

If I'd realized back then that my childish instincts and insights were correct, so many things would have been easier for me. And if I'd known that, years later, I'd find myself in a different reality and experience things that I'd only suspected could be real, my whole life would have turned out differently. But that wasn't the point. Today, as I'll explain later in the book, it makes a lot of sense that as a child I felt so torn, because those experiences were the *exact* ones I was so desperately seeking and needed.

Existing But Not Living

As I grew up, after a few teething problems, I dutifully learned how a person must behave if they want to earn their place in society and be respected. I was taught to adapt to what other people expected of me, and to meet their demands and needs. In time, I came to believe that to be loved and accepted, I had to spend all day, every day, in service to others. I constantly shifted my own boundaries to accommodate other people; I twisted and betrayed myself just to feel that I belonged; and I exhausted myself in a meritocratic society, overstepping my own limits just to feel worthy.

To lead an autonomous life, we must develop a healthy dose of self-confidence, but that's exactly what I *didn't* do. I lacked the courage to listen to and respond to my own needs, and as my life progressed I felt increasingly small, helpless, and powerless in the face of everything. Ultimately, in a bid to feel safe and secure, I attempted to control everything that was going on inside me and around me. As a result, I was constantly on guard, trying desperately hard not to offend anyone or to attract attention to myself.

Finally, I resigned myself to being lived by life instead of listening to my inner voice, and that voice became quieter and quieter until it was finally silenced. And that hurt.

After I got married and had two children, my relentless, ongoing fight against myself and the life that society had set out for me began to take its toll on my physical and mental state. I learned everything there is to know about feeling stuck and being miserable, from emotional self-destruction to depression. Although it wouldn't have been noticeable from the outside, my life was anything but fulfilling; in fact, the days dragged by, and the nights were filled with dread. I was deeply unhappy, but over the years, I'd successfully learned to suppress and disguise my feelings. I'd put on a mask and whenever someone asked me how I was, I'd reply with a rehearsed smile, 'Fine, thanks. And you?'

Eventually, I found myself living in a big house with my family. By then I'd become a workaholic, and although I earned enough money to buy anything my heart desired, inside I was burned out and empty, a hollow shell of a human being. Despite my outward success and status, I still felt worthless, helpless, and incredibly lost. I tried to hide behind everything and everyone, and more than anything, I longed to become invisible.

My fear of the noisy and demanding world outside me had become so unbearable over the years that I just wanted to get away from it. I needed some relief from the emptiness I felt inside, but I had nowhere to escape to. I'd successfully boxed myself in and saw neither a way out nor a solution for my situation. I was far too afraid of change.

However, on one seemingly ordinary autumn evening, my life *did* change – utterly. The change was so radical, so thorough, and so unexpected that if I'd had an inkling of what was about to happen, I'd have done everything, *anything*, possible to avoid it.

CHAPTER 2

A Very Personal
Wake-Up Call

I remember the events of September 28, 2009 very well, which is incredible because my memories of anything that happened before that date are hazy. As I've explained, my life back then was bleak and unfulfilling, and I was very unhappy, so when I think about what I experienced on, and after, that fateful autumn day, I feel extremely grateful because it presented me with the greatest and most meaningful gift imaginable.

A few weeks earlier, I'd found a fantastic way to alleviate my inner emptiness, at least temporarily: jogging. The only time I felt truly at peace and undisturbed was when I went for a jog. Pulling on my running gear became the perfect excuse to leave the house because no one asked what I was doing or why I was doing it. No one noticed that I was running away; no one knew how relieved I felt when I shut the front door and began my run.

As each stride took me further away from our house, an invisible burden would lift from my shoulders, and I'd feel freer. I'd often jog through the surrounding woodland, just to be certain I was completely alone and could stop pretending to everyone, and most of all, to myself. My mask came off, and that alone made me breathe more easily.

The truth is, I was afraid of myself. Increasingly often, I'd fantasize about just packing my belongings and running off – somewhere, anywhere, far, far away from everything I was thinking and feeling. However, there was such a void inside me that doing anything at all, however small, took all my strength.

Who am I really? I'd been asking myself that question for several weeks; over and over, it would pop into my head. It was even starting to appear as I jogged through the woods, which was when I was at my least tense, my most unburdened. On the afternoon of September 28, the words echoed in my mind as I ran: *I need to know who I really am.* This idea wasn't a new one to me, and usually I just pushed it aside; however, I was finding it more and more difficult to do so. How could I continue to live my life in this way? I was stuck in a terrible rut, and I knew that I had to get out of it.

By the time I returned home that day, dusk had fallen, and my body was chilled to the bone; I'd been out jogging for almost three hours. I was feeling exhausted yet empowered by the crucial realization that I couldn't go on like this. Something *had* to change, even if I didn't yet know what or how.

A Flaming Human Torch

I needed to warm up quickly, so without bothering to change out of my running gear, I headed straight to the living room to light a fire. After throwing a few logs in the fireplace, I poured on plenty of liquid firelighter, struck a match, and stood back. I don't remember exactly how it happened, but moments later I realized that the hem on one leg of my baggy sweatpants had caught alight.

Feeling a pang of annoyance at my carelessness, I beat at the flames with my bare hands, thinking I could put them out. But I was very wrong. Within seconds, both legs of my sweatpants were ablaze, the flames climbing relentlessly up my body. After an initial moment of shock, I used my hands once more, but the more I did so, the more easily the fire seemed to eat through the flimsy synthetic fabric of my running clothes.

It turned out that in my haste to get a fire started as quickly as possible, I'd grabbed a bottle of highly flammable bioethanol fuel instead of the safer liquid firelighter. Bioethanol consists of pure alcohol and the flames it produces are intense and very difficult to extinguish. A few drops off the mark, a small spark, and it can all end in disaster. And that's what happened to me; it seems I'd spilt some of the fuel on my clothes.

By now, the heat was unbearable, but still, I didn't scream or call out for help; in fact, I didn't utter a sound. *I can get this under control*, I thought. From today's perspective, this scenario was completely surreal, and my behavior seems odd, almost remote-controlled. Even when both my arms and my entire torso were on fire, it didn't occur to me to throw myself onto the ground or to run. It was only when the flames reached my face – I can still hear them crackling and hissing as they devoured my long, thick hair – that I realized I could *not* control the situation.

By this point, I was standing in the middle of our living room, fully alight like a human torch. Only then did I try to call for help. I attempted to take a deep breath to let out a desperate cry, but instead of the cool air I longed for, blistering heat poured into my mouth and throat. It was simply intolerable, and I suddenly understood that I'd left it too late.

What impresses me the most today is that I didn't feel any pain during all this, and I don't remember being afraid, either. I've since learned that when we sustain third-degree burns, we stop feeling pain because the nerve endings are destroyed and the agony that we should be experiencing far exceeds the body's pain scale.

But none of this really mattered to me then. As the moment arrived when I could no longer breathe, I thought, *I'm going to die.* And then I stopped fighting the thought and the feeling because there was simply nothing more that could be done. I made one of the most important decisions of my life: I gave up the fight. The fight against the fire, the fight against life, the fight against myself. I accepted the situation for what it was. End of.

Reflecting on My Experience

Now, many years later, it's still difficult for me to describe that moment. It was made up of everything and nothing all at once. Perfect inner calm, a peaceful silence, and a full *surrender* to whatever would come next. It taught me what 'letting go' really means – it's not about *doing* anything; it's about *letting* things happen. You stop fighting, you stop resisting, and you surrender to your circumstances. I once had trouble understanding how to let go. I always thought I had to do something, realize something, or change things; but instead, it's simply a matter of letting go of the very thing we're trying to hold on to.

Many people who have had a near-death experience report that their life flashed before their eyes, but that didn't happen to me. Instead, I knew with absolute certainty that the life that I'd lived was right and good, just as it had been. Despite all the dark, negative emotions and thoughts that had taken up so much space within me, I felt neither grief nor regret. There was nothing to do, nowhere to be, but simply a *point*.

Everything that had been significant in my life until then lost all meaning. None of it *really* mattered. None of it was *really* as bad or as dramatic as I'd portrayed it. I'd made my life difficult for nothing – struggling and fighting against things which, in the face of impending death, no longer held any importance.

I realized that it didn't matter how successful I'd been in my career. It didn't matter how much I'd sacrificed – for whatever reason. It didn't matter whether I was liked by other people or how well I'd pretended to function. In that moment, which lasted for one or two breaths but felt like an eternity, everything was fine just the way it was. Without any judgment. I was ready to close the door on my life and let go of everything that had ever mattered to me.

I could write page after page about what was happening inside me as I received these profound insights. It was a magical moment in which I placed myself completely – and most importantly, *consciously* – into the hands of a higher power. I relinquished all control and fully surrendered. And then there was a peaceful, almost curious, wait for what would follow, come what may.

Detaching from My Body

There I stood, all 5ft 8 of me, fully ablaze with 10-foot-high flames roaring all around me. I could no longer breathe, no longer move my body, and I'd missed the opportunity to call for help. The last thing I was consciously aware of was the relentlessness of the fire as it consumed me inside my own personal hell.

But then, something very strange indeed happened. Suddenly, as if I'd been catapulted out of my body, I was able to see myself from the *outside*. One second, I was in my body and the next I'd become detached from it, although I was still fully conscious and alert. I could still feel the intense heat of the fire, still smell the stench of my scorched clothes and burning hair, and still see the flames licking the charred ceiling, except now I was experiencing it all from a spot some six feet away from my body.

A peculiar sense of neutrality set in as I watched my burning body, like a casual bystander amidst the chaos. Slowly, it began to stagger and flail its arms helplessly; it couldn't continue like this for much longer, I realized.

My dispassion suddenly turned to joy when I saw my son appear in the doorway of the living room. As fast as lightning, 14-year-old Manuel grasped that this was a life-threatening situation and he acted instinctively, yelling loudly for help and at the same time lunging at my body and pulling it to the floor. Without hesitating for even a second, he risked his own life to save mine.

Alerted by Manuel's cries, my friend Moni and her daughter rushed into the room. They, too, immediately understood how much danger I was in and, pulling Manuel to one side, they smothered the fire by dragging a large rug over my body. Looking on from outside my body, I watched their fight to save my life with fascination rather than terror. I was in a very strange state, for which I simply cannot find the right words. Neutral, interested, observing, curious... they all fit, but none of them really capture the feeling.

After the greatest danger had been averted, Moni instructed Manuel to call an ambulance while she and her daughter carried my limp body into the bathroom. How they managed to lift me into my huge bathtub is a mystery, because I was certainly of no help. While Moni showered my face and hands with cold water, her daughter carefully removed the rings from my fingers, which had already fused into the skin; neither of them attempted to pull the scorched clothes from my charred body. I remember the look of sheer horror on their faces as they did these things, and today, I applaud them for the amazing foresight they demonstrated.

The Silent Observer

'Anke, open your eyes! Open your eyes and tell me if you can see me. Anke, please! Talk to me,' Moni cried as she continued to shower my skin, concentrating especially on my burned face. The shock of the ice-cold water and Moni's desperate words pulled me out of unconsciousness very briefly, and my awareness returned to my body. I tried to open my eyes and took a deep, conscious breath, tasting the water in my mouth, before I was pulled out of my body again.

From a distance, I watched as three paramedics rushed into the bathroom carrying all their equipment. They cut open my sweatpants and running jacket and peeled strips of charred material from my body so they could treat my wounds as best they could. When they were done, they carried my motionless body into the ambulance that was waiting in front of the house and handed me over to an emergency doctor.

Fortunately for me, the doctor immediately recognized the severity of my injuries and radioed for a rescue helicopter to take me to a hospital as quickly as possible. (I found out later that she'd worked for three years in the intensive care unit of a specialist clinic for burns patients in Munich, southern

Germany. She could have taken me to the University Hospital Regensburg in just a few minutes as it was close to my home, but she decided against it. Instead, she contacted her old colleagues in the Munich clinic and was told there was just one bed available in the intensive care unit.)

When she made the radio call, the doctor was informed that a rescue helicopter was flying over the highway just five minutes away and it would be able to take us to Munich. The flying intensive care unit landed on the football pitch in our town, where the ambulance had relocated and was ready and waiting. All these actions that came together so seamlessly to get me into the hands of the medical specialists were nothing short of a miracle, and knowing this still fills me with the deepest gratitude.

Caught Between Life and Death

In the helicopter, I watched the nice emergency doctor keep a constant watch over my readings in a calm, reassuring way. I saw her fill in forms and carefully look after my charred body, which from my vantage point appeared to be in a deep sleep. I didn't have the capacity to fully grasp the extent of my burns – not that I really cared. I saw – and smelled – the black, charred skin on my face and hands. I noticed the fabric that had partially melted into my skin, and I could still feel the heat of the fire in my throat.

However, I felt very comfortable in the strange neutral state I'd been in since I'd left my body. I read later that this state often occurs at the moment of death, when the person's consciousness detaches from the physical body, ready to leave this earthly plane. The consciousness then lingers close to the body until the process of cutting the cord is complete, and only then does it move on to the next realm.

But this was different. While my consciousness *had* detached from my body, and I lingered next to it like a spectator or a cohabitor, the cord wasn't cut. Nothing drew me fully from my body. There were no long-dead relatives welcoming me lovingly to the next life. There was no bright light to follow, no dark tunnel. There was nothing like that at all.

The calm atmosphere in the helicopter was beneficial to me, and having some time and space on the journey enabled me to come to terms with my peculiar situation a little better. Things only became hectic again when we landed in Munich and the paramedics took my body from the helicopter to the hospital.

Doctors hurried over and I was rushed to the intensive care unit. Bottles, tubes, and a folder lay on my stomach, but from my position outside my body, I seemed fine. I looked as if I was simply in a deep, relaxing sleep, and all the commotion that was happening around me was a total mystery.

I heard the emergency doctor give a report on my condition to her colleagues and watched as my body was taken to an examination room. The thing that puzzled me, though, was that nobody took any notice of me. The whole time I lay in that brightly lit room, surrounded by doctors and nurses busily tending to my body as they put me in a medically induced coma, nobody answered any of my questions.

They didn't seem to hear me, and that just didn't make sense to me. I was right there! I wanted to know what was happening to my body, but no one spoke to me. What were the doctors doing to it? And why did they look so worried?

It took me quite some time to realize that no one on this human level could perceive me. Not my son in the living room, nor the doctor in the helicopter, and most certainly not the frantic doctors and other medical staff at the hospital. Even though at the time I didn't understand why this was, I eventually gave in to the situation in which I'd found myself and returned to the more enjoyable role of silent observer.

Chapter 3

Am I Dead?

As my body lay motionless in the hospital bed, I took the opportunity to look at it a little more closely, and in peace, for the first time since the helicopter journey. I'd been moved to a quiet two-bed room with magnolia walls in the intensive care unit, and from my vantage point at the foot of the bed, it appeared that I was being cared for very well, with devices monitoring my vital signs and tubes supplying me with everything I needed to survive.

It felt very strange indeed to be able to observe myself from the outside like this; after all, we don't usually get to see ourselves the way others do. As my body lay there like an empty shell – vacant and lifeless – my spirit was detached from it, but not completely. Confused thoughts ran through my mind: *What does all this mean? Why don't I feel what my body feels? If I'm dead, then why am I still here? Why am I still attached to my body? What am I waiting for?*

On the one hand, it seemed quite natural that I'd left my body, but on the other, the distance felt odd. I felt no pain, no pressure, and even less fear. What I *did* feel, however, was a kind of expansion; a freedom that I'd never experienced before in my life. Everything felt so wonderfully light, as if the weight of the world had been lifted from my shoulders.

But then slowly, another feeling crept in – puzzlement – and with it came more questions and doubts. *Why can't anyone see or hear me? I'm right here, for God's sake, and I feel as fresh as a daisy!* I found myself becoming preoccupied by strange thoughts: *What on earth is this? I must be dead – there's no other explanation – but if I'm dead then why has nothing changed?*

I also felt as if I was waiting peacefully for something, although I didn't know what it was. It was a highly disconcerting situation, one that's very difficult to imagine if you haven't experienced it yourself. But try to put yourself in my shoes.

Free as a Bird

I felt no connection to my body whatsoever; it didn't even feel like it belonged to me. It was as if my body itself was home to all the pain, sadness, and heaviness of the previous few years of my life, whereas I finally felt free of it all, unburdened at last. I couldn't remember ever feeling so free and light. I was like a bird that's spent its life in a tiny cage and has suddenly been set free. But now that the cage door was open, I didn't really know what to do with my freedom.

I began by looking around the room. The smell of disinfectant was overpowering, and at the head of the two beds were numerous medical devices, all switched on. Aside from their constant beeping, however, there was utter silence. An elderly lady lay in the bed next to mine. She, too, seemed to be asleep and was smiling blissfully as she dreamed.

As I began to wonder why she was smiling, I suddenly found myself in her dream. I was in a beautiful ballroom with giant crystal chandeliers hanging from the ceiling, illuminating the scene with a radiant light. I could hear music playing and my eyes fell on a beautiful young woman in a breathtaking cream ball gown. She was safe in the arms of a man who looked at her lovingly as he led her around the room in a waltz.

The couple appeared to be oblivious to the people around them and only had eyes for each other. They were one with themselves, the music, and their bodies, and nothing else seemed to matter. I understood why the old lady was smiling and seemed so happy, even though her body was asleep. The moment I'd found myself wondering why she was smiling, I'd become immersed in her inner experience, just as if it were my own. It was as if she and I were connected in some strange but magical way.

Meeting My Teacher

Meanwhile, the hospital had become quieter; every now and then I heard someone walking along the corridor from one room to another, the murmur of doctors talking to each other, and the soft whirring of the medical equipment. I was still trying to wrap my mind around my bizarre situation and what had happened, when the atmosphere and conditions around me suddenly and dramatically altered.

The room expanded, becoming much bigger than before, and it was filled with immaterial and intangible things. Everything was permeated by an endless spectrum of colors. The vibration and light changed, too, making all the objects in the room seem brighter and softer. Surprised by this abrupt transformation, I glanced around, and as I did so, a very odd feeling came over me. Something strange was going on.

'Everything is OK, Anke.' A soft, melodious voice carried through the room.

Startled, I turned in the direction that I thought the voice was coming from and saw a radiant figure smiling invitingly at me. It was as high as the ceiling and the light it emanated was so indescribably bright that I could barely make out a body. I stood spellbound beside the bed for what felt like an eternity, staring at the figure.

I'd never seen anything so beautiful. This figure made of soft celestial light had the power to change everything it touched. The walls, and every object within those walls, were suddenly transparent; everything material seemed to change its density in the presence of this being.

The figure, the presence, was more than just light, and more than a spectrum of colors. As I slowly regained my composure, it moved cautiously and respectfully toward me, tilting its head slightly. Now that it was closer, I sensed that the figure was emanating a somewhat masculine energy. I immediately felt safe and protected because it felt as if he knew me.

'Are you here to take me?' I asked, still dumbfounded. 'Because I'm dead?'

'Not at all,' he replied encouragingly. 'There's nothing to be afraid of. All your questions will be answered soon. Nothing here matters right now, so I'd like to show you a few things, if that's OK with you.'

Did I want that? *Definitely*. Nothing would have made me happier. I finally realized what I'd been waiting for. I was no longer alone, and maybe I'd receive some answers to my many questions. As the figure came closer still, I could feel myself being drawn into his luminous energy field. And then I was gone.

PART II

To the Source and Back

CHAPTER 4

The Journey Begins

As the light figure drew me away, I heard his reassuring words: 'You can trust me. Just let go and complete the transformation.' The first thing I noticed was that I was immediately able to let go of everything that had been weighing me down for so many years, and this freedom felt unbelievably good. The physical, material environment that had upset me so much, as well as my body and everything that had happened to me so far in my life, became increasingly less important.

My numerous thoughts dissolved into nothingness as I was drawn out of the room, out of the hospital, and away from all that had been so real to me. Suddenly, everything felt infinitely light, almost vibrational, and the further away we got, the more natural it seemed that I found myself in this new, miraculous state. The more I let myself go and gave in to the vibration of the light-filled presence that surrounded me so protectively, the more detached I felt.

I had the extraordinary sense that I was no longer bound by structure or material density. It was like an inner liberation, and I felt a happiness that I'd never experienced in my life. I felt completely safe embedded in this energy field, in this unlimited space bound by a great, unconditional love. It was pulling me higher and higher – or at least that's how it seemed, because I'd already lost awareness of space and time.

It even felt as if I was *becoming* this unlimited space – that my consciousness was expanding into it further and further. I felt freer, lighter, and more alive than ever before. Nothing scared me, even though I didn't know what was happening and where it would lead me. But what I did know was that I was on an incredible journey. *If this is what happens to us when we die,* I thought, *I don't know why I was ever afraid of it.*

A Universal Consciousness

I was so overwhelmed by my newfound sense of freedom that I didn't notice we were slowing down. The unlimited space around us began to change as we entered realms crafted from a brilliant, fluorescent light – a light so bright that it almost blinded me. It wasn't light as we know it on Earth; it wasn't simply that it shone brightly but rather that it was made up of an infinite number of colors and frequencies, arranged in a way that made it feel alive.

I could not only see this light but also feel it and experience it with all my senses. It felt limitless, as if it was coming from nowhere and everywhere at the same time. The light brought out in me overwhelming yet glorious feelings and sensations. I wish I could make you experience them too and help you to tap into them within yourself. I wish I were a painter so I could use all those cosmic colors to create a picture of everything I saw, learned, and felt, so you could get a true sense of what I'm telling you.

It's the light of a living, universal consciousness that permeates everything in existence. It makes you feel a complete, pure, and *unconditional love* – none of the emotions we experience as human beings come even close to it.

It was truly amazing – the more I opened myself up to this living consciousness, the more I was able to immerse myself in its all-embracing love. There were no limits, and everywhere I looked, I could see nothing but heavenly light. Suddenly, I felt ground beneath my feet; we appeared to have reached our destination.

There was a floor that wasn't a real floor, and yet it was there. It was beneath feet that I no longer had, and yet I still felt them. A very familiar yet wonderful feeling. Only then did I realize that I still identified with my body in the way I always had, although so much had changed. I still felt like myself, an autonomous individual with my own thoughts and feelings, and although I knew that I'd left my physical body behind in the hospital, I was somehow standing on two legs and examining my transparent hands.

Am I dead, then? Who are you? I thought you were going to answer all my... I hadn't even fully thought this last question when I sensed that the protective presence surrounding me had shifted and he was now right in front of me. Entire worlds were reflected in his golden-yellow light when I was able to look at it a little more closely for the first time. The figure was magical; everything about him drew me in and felt so familiar.

'You're not dead! Let go, Anke. Let it all go,' he said. His words felt like the most loving embrace, to which I gratefully succumbed.

I have so many questions, I thought. His reassuring answer came immediately: 'I know. All your questions will be answered. We'll explain everything to you and show you all that you need to see. But let go now, Anke. Just take in the light and get used to its frequencies. Everything will come at the right time. You'll soon understand.'

Bound by Unconditional Love

The more I let go and let in this universal consciousness, the more I understood that everything in this spiritual realm was different from what I'd previously believed. As soon as you think a thought, everything it entails is thought into existence simultaneously. When a question arises, so do all its possible answers. Feelings, as we know them, don't exist, because any human emotion falls far short of this comprehensive awareness.

Nothing in the spiritual realm is directed toward a single person or situation; everything permeates everything else. It's a state of being – an all-encompassing state that's underpinned by unconditional love. Time as we know it in the material world is completely absent – everything's happening right now and therefore all at once. As soon as you turn your attention to it, you perceive everything that ever was and ever will be, simultaneously.

I was fascinated by all this. I'd suspected that everything in the universe must be connected in some way, but the further I extended my own consciousness into the spiritual realm in which I now found myself, the more I was able to grasp the complex synchronicity that exists. What I didn't know then was that I was in the process of consciously connecting with the vibration of my soul.

Reflecting on My Experience

Today I know that what we humans think of as real has very little to do with our actual reality. We look at our bodies and perceive them as physical matter; we look at our environment and think it's static, fixed, and permanent; we look at our lives without paying much attention to the miracles that are taking place all around us; we look at the people around us without grasping that we're connected to them, that we're one with them.

We feel separate from everything within us and around us. But as I'll show you in this book, this is an illusion – a fatal error of perception that lays the foundation for our entire, very limited, view of the world. It's like holding a handful of sand and being convinced it's the entire desert. As humans, we're bound to space and time by our three-dimensional vibrational frequency, so we perceive that all events take place in a chronological order. We only have the capacity to concentrate on a single point in time, and to do this we have to block out everything else. So, we labor under the illusion that a past and a future exist, and that we don't have access to higher levels of consciousness. And due to our perception that we're isolated, separate individuals, even if we do sense that everything's connected in some way, we're unable to grasp the bigger picture.

The soul, however, is a multidimensional field of consciousness that can register everything simultaneously – multidimensionally – and vibrate at a much higher frequency. During my journey to the spiritual realm, I experienced my soul as the link between the unconscious and the very Source from which it originates.

The soul isn't subject to space and time, and yet it permeates them completely because the soul is the Source of our consciousness. Our soul stores all our experiences from previous lives, and it knows our higher purpose and path, our current life plan and all the challenges – and the solutions to those challenges – that come with it. (You'll discover more about the illusion of separation and our personal life plan later in the book.)

CHAPTER 5

Hindsight

'Let go, Anke. Let it all go.' My companion's voice echoed within me, filling me with a current of deep love that went hand in hand with his words. Nothing can compare to the joy and happiness I experienced then, nor the wondrous feeling of 'coming home.'

Although I refer to him as 'he,' the light figure wasn't necessarily male; as I mentioned earlier, some of his qualities felt male to me, but at the same time, others were female. All I know is that 'he' possessed every quality I associate with love. I felt his infinite wisdom, his endless compassion, and all that I imagine goodness to be. But the most wonderful thing was the incredible love he had for me. I'd never felt so loved, and in such an unconditional, appreciative, and personal way; it still moves me today.

The light figure allowed me to adjust and adapt to the intensity of his energy field. I was fully aware that he was allowing me to share in just a small fraction of his frequency, as I probably wouldn't have been able to bear the full extent of it. But there was one thing I was certain of in that moment: I *never* wanted to leave him or this place.

As I gradually became used to his energy, the figure slowly began to teach me, primarily using the universal language of telepathy. We did talk, theoretically, and when I didn't understand something, he used images to explain it to me: as I watched in awe, vast picture libraries would fan out into multidimensional holograms.

He knew what I was thinking before I'd even thought it, and the answers I received from him were often so extensive, complex, and multilayered that understanding them pushed me to the edge of comprehension. As a human, I was used to seeing things three-dimensionally, but it seemed that in the spiritual realm, the possibilities were unlimited when it came to conveying knowledge and learning. Everything I saw, I could also *feel* at the same time, which enabled me to expand my perspective with ease.

Seeing the Connections

Once I'd become somewhat accustomed to my teacher's frequency, the first thing he showed me was a 'review' of my life to date. I saw the key events of my childhood; all the occasions when I'd tried to understand the world around me and had marveled as things opened out before me at breakneck speed.

I observed myself as a curious little girl with a zest for life, and an impetuous desire to try everything and anything she possibly could. I saw myself as a child who asked thousands of questions and had an unerring sense that the world around her was like a great adventure playground. And there and then, in that expanded consciousness, I was given the opportunity to obtain the answers to all my childhood questions in a single moment.

Situations and events that had occurred in my early and later years continued to appear rapidly before me, merging into one another, and this perspective allowed me to grasp that they were all connected. Suddenly, I was overwhelmed by the realization that everything that had happened to me had done so in accordance with a higher purpose.

*Nothing exists separately as a sole
entity, and absolutely everything is
connected to everything else.*

I was shown that even seemingly insignificant events had been a piece in a bigger picture and found that I could identify a deeper meaning behind incidents I'd long forgotten about or had dismissed as a one-off. For example, I saw myself shortly after starting school, sitting in the classroom feeling and looking very unsure of myself. I was afraid of the other children and overwhelmed by the pressure that comes with this big development in a child's life. I could sense that I felt I'd been forced into situations I'd rather have avoided but wasn't allowed to.

And this was *exactly* the way I'd felt – almost all the time – as an adult, culminating in the powerlessness and emptiness I'd experienced shortly before my accident. On countless occasions, I'd tried desperately to resolve my insecurities but to no avail. Now I understood that the events of my childhood and those of my later years were connected, and I gained a new perspective on my life and its purpose.

Everything Everywhere at Once

The more willing I became to expand my consciousness in this way, the more extensive my luminous companion made the training. He showed me the most complex connections between individual, apparently distinct, life events, revealing again and again their deeper meaning. And all of this was presented with an unbelievable clarity and intricacy that still inspires me when I think back on it.

Let me try to explain this to you in a different way. Imagine that you're sitting in a vast round room surrounded by multiple screens. Each screen shows a particular stage of your life, like a scene in a movie. But you don't just watch a *visual* review of your life; you're also aware of all the feelings and thoughts you have in each scene. And you also grasp the connection between the specific events of your life because you recognize what happened subsequently *because* of them.

It wouldn't be possible for our limited human mind to process all this data at once – certainly not the multidimensionality of the images I was shown. It would be like focusing our attention on all the screens in the room simultaneously, fully comprehending every single event down to the tiniest detail.

Parental Bonds and Past Lives

After my astonishment had subsided a little, my teacher directed my gaze to other, higher-level connections between the events of my life. I felt I was being allowed to dive deeper and deeper into a truth that could only be understood incrementally. It was as if I now had the opportunity to look at the meaning of my life from a spiritual perspective.

As I continued to watch the scenes from my life play out, I saw many in which I was at my mother's side as she modelled certain emotions and behaviors to me, among them fear and powerlessness. But now I could also recognize her soul. I felt her unconditional love for me and gained an insight into her higher purpose, which she fulfilled for me as my mother. I saw our loving bond and our earthly interaction as mother and daughter.

To help me better understand these spiritual connections with my mother, I was then shown scenes from the countless other lives that she and I had spent together. She hadn't always been my mother; she'd taken on different roles in many of her own lives and was an important person for me in most of my lives, too.

In one scene, I recognized her as my younger brother, with whom I shared the burden of responsibility in a very difficult family situation. When we were both very young, we had to take care of our sick mother while suffering at the hands of our cold, merciless father whose anger was relentless and uncontrolled – he'd lash out at anything in his path.

My brother and I were constantly on guard, trying to protect our mother by drawing our father's attention to us instead of her. The images of this past life and the memories they evoked made me feel profoundly sad. I'd been my little brother's only support, and when I'd died at the hands of my father, he'd been left all alone.

How often in my current life had I misunderstood my mother? How often had I been angry with her when she was powerless or afraid of something of which I was unaware? So much of our mutual behavior made sense to me when I understood these connections. Everything I'd ever struggled to understand about our relationship fell away when I realized our soul tasks for one another.

One of the challenges that my mother wanted to take on in this life was resolving her fears and the associated sense of powerlessness. And I needed help with these same issues myself; my teacher showed me that the personal challenge I'd chosen for this life was to experience unconditional love for myself, so my mother and I were ideal teachers for one other.

When I was a young girl, my mother's experience served as a model for me to develop feelings of fear and helplessness, and then to find ways to break free of them as my life progressed. In turn, I always challenged my mother to come into her power and move past her self-imposed limits. Realizing this allowed me to reframe our connection. We weren't merely mother and daughter, we weren't only intertwined on a spiritual level or through our different experiences. We were one. We came from the same Source.

A Perfect Teacher

The meaning behind this realization became even clearer to me when my luminous companion showed me my connections with my father. Here, too, I perceived first and foremost the unconditional love we held for each other on a spiritual level. However, paradoxically, he'd also been the person in my life who had inflicted my severest emotional wounds.

I'd always measured my worth in relation to my father, and he'd been my greatest teacher. The openness, spontaneity, and curiosity I'd displayed as a child had come from him. He'd always pushed me to think outside the box, taught me to go beyond my limits and to seek out the meaning behind everything life threw at me. However, at the same time, he'd also stifled my self-awareness and my sense that I was unique; ultimately, he didn't encourage me to have positive feelings about myself. This behavior had taught me that I was inferior and powerless.

Whether we'd fought or loved one another, my father and I had always been bound by mutual respect. For example, I watched scenes in which as scientists, we were engaged in very similar research on the laws of nature. We viewed each other with suspicion and tried to sabotage one another's work; and we focused our energy on competition rather than collaboration, which would have been far more productive.

Throughout our many past lives together my father and I were competitors, opponents, or teachers for one other. I was struck by the fact that we always seemed to spur each other on and inspire each other – just as we'd done in this life.

From my vantage point in the spiritual realm, I realized how perfectly all my early experiences, some of them very traumatic, were woven into what my teacher called my 'personal life plan' and fitted with my goal of achieving unconditional love for myself.

Writing Our Own Story

My teacher seemed to take great pleasure in showing me the higher purpose of all those who had played a significant role in my life – not just my parents, but my husband and children and many other people who had influenced me. From this perspective, all these individuals were like the cast of the film of my life, in which I played the leading role.

The people closest to us, those who have a strong influence and impact on our lives, are, from a spiritual perspective, part of us. We're here for many of the same reasons and we're bound together in unconditional love. All the difficulties and challenges that we experience through other people are in fact gifts that – without exception – help us to grow and develop, bringing with them the treasure of self-knowledge. We're like a group of performers who enjoy staging new stories time and time again. We direct tragedies and comedies, writing in love or action scenes, and top it all off with a good dose of drama. And we're all writing the scripts of our lives, together.

Everyone is the main character in their own story, and everyone plays a key supporting role in everyone else's story. But that's not to say we always play the same role; in the long run that would be boring and deprive us of experience. So, we swap stories and switch roles among ourselves, together developing elaborate life plans so that we can all experience exactly what we want to experience.

I was deeply moved when I realized how carefully things have been aligned in this way; how they fit together perfectly and make sense – for every one of us. It was clear that my accident and this spiritual layover with my teacher was part of my bigger life plan, although I was still a long way from being able to see it fully.

> *When the invisible becomes visible, you*
> *can never fall back into ignorance.*

Realizing how small and insignificant our life is in terms of the vastness of our spiritual existence felt incredible and it helped me enormously in broadening my perspective. It was especially enlightening to know that we're all connected to one other on a higher spiritual level. For me, understanding that there's no separation, no distinction, that not only are we all connected but we all come from the same Source, was huge.

Reflecting on My Experience

Before I learned about the bonds that we all share or knew anything of the higher purpose of all that's happened in my life, I'd been fighting against my reality. Subconsciously, I'd spent my life feeling like a victim of external circumstances. However, I found peace when I realized that my parents and I had entered the game of life together in love, diving headfirst into all its challenges to create opportunities for each other to grow.

Almost instantly, I stopped struggling against them and gave way to a state of total recognition. I realized that all the resistance I'd felt inside was never really directed at the outside world; in fact, I'd been fighting against myself. Knowing that my parents had not only given me their DNA, love, wisdom, and foresight, but also all the challenges I needed to grow, was a huge weight off my shoulders.

And I realized that although they'd given me all these things, they were only the basic prerequisites that allowed me to face and overcome my greatest challenges. All my suffering, frustration, and anger at the world in which I lived had a purpose – *my* purpose. These were the very experiences I needed to have and which I'd chosen for myself for this life. My parents had merely 'enabled' me.

Equally, I recognized myself as a valuable part of my parents' life plan and this was just as eye-opening. My rebellion against pressure, restriction, and fear also provided my mother and father with countless opportunities to grow. I was exactly what they needed, and they were just what I needed, simply by being the way we are. I bowed before them in love and gave them the recognition they deserved.

All Part of the Plan

For me, the realization that every situation we encounter in our lives – whether fortunate or less so – is in accordance with a higher purpose was overwhelming. Everything that happens is part of a perfectly formulated plan, and in my life, I was always where I needed to be because I myself had chosen to be there.

> *Nothing happens by chance.*
> *Nothing happens without our input.*
> *Nothing is against us; we have no opponents.*

Having said that, I was also shown that I'd had a pretty elaborate plan for this life before I was even born. There was so much I wanted to know, learn, and experience in a human body; I didn't want to cut corners or compromise, so I decided to go for the extremes. Radical experiences, extreme challenges, and the greatest happiness were the order of the day because that was the only way to somehow accommodate my long list of wishes for this life.

I could have chosen countless other souls to be my mother and father, but my parents were just right for me and for my ambitious project. They, too, intended to live a life of extremes and wanted a child to support them in that. So, laughing and buzzing with joyful anticipation, we worked out our life plans together. We allowed some flexibility and space for the unexpected, and for us to make our own decisions and go at our own pace, but the cornerstones were set.

And for me personally, there was one particularly important point: Since I didn't know before I was born whether I'd get lost in this game of extremes, I built myself a kind of safety net. If I lost my way in life, no matter when it was, this would get me back on track. I'll tell you how my teacher helped me to remember that I'd done this in Chapter 11.

CHAPTER 6

The Illusion of Loneliness

Learning about the intricate connections and the higher purpose behind everything was so exciting. It felt like a revelation. All this information and all these insights were deeply fulfilling. I felt connected and as if I'd fully come home to myself. If my spiritual teacher had ended our journey together at this point, it still would have been more than worth it in every respect.

'What role do you play in this game?' I felt the question arise in me; it was one I'd not yet asked the limitless field of energy who had made all this possible. 'If we're all there for each other and there to support one another as we seek out the experiences that we've chosen for ourselves, then what part do you play? Who *are* you and why do I feel such a strong connection to you?'

As if he'd been waiting for me to ask this very question, my teacher answered, laughing, 'Are you ready to take a big step forward? Are you ready to see yourself for who you really are?'

'Am I ready for that? Of course I am!' I replied, laughing too.

He began by showing me my current life, but in a completely different way than he'd done previously, once more giving me enough space to take it all in, step by step. Although I could still understand and categorize the bonds I shared with my family and other people around me, I now saw everything from the neutral perspective of an observer, as if I were a bird calmly looking down on the entire landscape below.

Every second of my life appeared in chronological order – from my birth to my 'death,' all the way through to the present moment – and I could follow it all as if watching a movie. I scrutinized the circumstances of my birth and my accident particularly closely. I saw that when I was born, I'd been unable to breathe by myself; my tiny body had emerged blue from my mother's womb, and my first breath had taken what little strength I had. I saw the doctors in the delivery room, deep in concentration and fighting for my life, just as other doctors were doing right now following my accident.

We're Never Alone

From my elevated viewpoint, I recognized a very special commonality between my birth and my 'death': the presence of the golden-yellow light of my teacher, which seemed to fill the entire space. Whether in the delivery room in Frankfurt at the beginning of my life or in my living room in front of the fireplace at its apparent end, the light was the same.

This realization hit me like a ton of bricks. 'You were there both times?' I gasped.

'I'm always there,' he answered in a calm, clear voice.

In the same moment, images of countless other events in my life played out, showing me in no uncertain terms that this light had always been by my side. Sometimes I sensed it close to me and other times it was further away, but it was always there.

Just when I felt I'd identified a beginning and an end to my current life, my teacher unveiled further glimpses of the countless other lives that I'd already lived, repeating with a smile, 'I'm always there!' Once more, I was simultaneously amazed and speechless. I recognized him immediately: In every single one of my incredibly different lives, my teacher's unmistakable golden light had been by my side.

I finally understood why he'd seemed so familiar to me from the very start of my journey. This unique feeling of 'coming home' and our love for each other was something both obvious and natural. We just knew one another so well. No matter what I'd experienced, no matter what challenges I'd had to overcome, he'd always been by my side, watching over me and helping me so that I never lost myself completely. Even now, as I write these words, I'm once again filled with that incomprehensible, all-embracing love and connection that my teacher revealed to me in that magical moment. I can feel his warm smile and the vibration in my cells that always lets me know he's nearby.

I'd barely had time to digest all this before my teacher directed my gaze to the many deaths I'd also experienced. At each one, he'd helped me to detach my consciousness from my body so I could enter the spiritual realm. Enveloping me in his infinite love, he'd helped me to let go of the burden of the life I'd just ended. Just as he'd done in this life.

Smiling, he said, 'You'll come to understand that I'm much more than you think. I'm not a person or an individual entity. I'm a part of you, I'm a part of your family, and at the same time I'm connected to everything that makes you who you are.

Oneness

My consciousness attempted to grasp and interpret what I was seeing and, most of all, what I was feeling with his words, but with the revelation that came next, my strength left me. I watched in amazement as the face, then the entire form and vibration, of my wise, loving, and familiar teacher transformed before my eyes. Suddenly, there was something powerful, majestic, and sublime in his voice and I was seized by a powerful wave of energy that brought me to my knees.

'I'll show you who we really are, Anke.' My teacher's words felt like an echo from within as he proceeded to merge with me completely. From that moment, 'I' ceased to exist. I could no longer tell whether he was showing me his world or immersing himself in my reality because all boundaries had been dissolved. There was no more 'he,' no more 'me,' no more 'above' or 'below,' no more past lives or other souls.

Everything I'd ever thought of as 'outside' of me
was united within me. I was everything all at
once. Everything that ever was and ever will be.

How could I ever have felt lonely, abandoned by God, punished? All those years I'd spent feeling unhappy with myself could only have been the result of forgetting this spiritual connection. Once more, I struggle to fully convey this limitless consciousness in which I found myself. So, to explain it to you in a way that you can hopefully understand, I'd like to alter your perspective for a moment.

The Drop of Blood

Imagine that you're a drop of blood on the tip of your right index finger. Everything you are, everything you believe about yourself, and everything you've ever experienced is contained in that drop of blood. You *are* that drop of blood, and everything else is outside of you.

Now imagine a vast, universal ocean made of pure consciousness. The ocean contains every single experience, vibration, and frequency in our universe and far beyond. It contains everything that we humans are already aware of, but also everything that we're not aware of and never can be. Everything that you think is outside you – the environment, other people, your soul, God – is in this ocean.

Now see yourself, as that drop of blood, slowly dripping from the tip of your finger into the ocean. Breaking off from the fingertip that's given you support and security until now, you consciously let yourself slip into the universal ocean of pure consciousness.

The moment you make contact with the water, you begin to transform. It's impossible for you to remain a drop of blood after you've mixed with the ocean and dissolved in it. Everything that you previously considered 'yours' no longer exists in this form. You yourself have become something much greater.

You're now the ocean, connected with everything it contains, your consciousness interwoven with cosmic consciousness. There's no longer any difference between you and it; you've become one. The ocean ceased to exist in the same way once you dripped into it. It's changed you, but you've also changed it and enhanced it with your qualities.

Close your eyes for a moment and *feel*. Imagine yourself as this drop of blood I've described. Think about everything you believe you know about yourself – your past, your experiences, your body. Everything that makes you who you are is contained in this drop of blood. You *are* this drop of blood. Now imagine yourself slowly dripping into a vast ocean that contains all of Creation. Feel how you connect with the water, how you dissolve in it and expand in it.

We all come from this oneness. We've all heard of it, maybe you even know a lot about it, but to experience it fully is impossible as long as we exist within the confines of a human body. You can only begin to understand this connection through feeling, and even then, only if you go beyond what you already know and enter the all-encompassing state in which I found myself.

Reflecting on My Experience

A few months after my accident, I began to search in various books for an explanation of what I'd experienced while in a coma. I read about soul families, spirit guides, and God, and through that I began to understand things to a certain extent.

Then, in a book about quantum physics, I discovered a couple of relatively easy-to-digest explanations of spacelessness and timelessness, heightened consciousness, and the idea that life is a field of infinite possibilities. These helped me to comprehend and process some of what had happened to me, but there's a huge difference between *believing* that there's much more to you than meets the eye and actually *experiencing* it.

What I experienced in the spiritual realm extends far beyond the limits of the human intellect. Getting to grips with such concepts as infinity or eternity is enormously challenging. In our mind, there must always be a beginning and an end, a before and an after; so, the truth is outside our understanding. However, if we ever did learn the truth about these concepts, our brains would shut down because we wouldn't be able to question anything, to classify and organize things into categories like higher or lower, bigger or smaller. We'd have to surrender to this all-encompassing *oneness*, and our habitual compartmentalization of things would cease.

One of the most wonderful changes that occurred after my near-death experience was that my mind surrendered, allowing me to stay connected to this limitless awareness. Since then – and it's been more than 10 years now – this state has been informing my life. It's always there for me to tap into whenever I choose, and I've been aware of my teacher's presence the entire time.

Everything Is Open to Us

After I returned to my body and my life, I presumed that my teacher would continue to answer all my questions and give me advice, and that I only needed to ask him when there was a decision to be made. But that wasn't the case – he was always there by my side, smiling, but he left me to figure things out on my own.

He didn't advise me on any of the countless decisions I had to make after my return; not once did he help me to figure out what was right or wrong for me. Mostly, he just showed me all the options available to me, and subsequently, he was happy about my choice – no matter what I chose. (I talk about all this in the Rebirth and Renewal section.)

I didn't always love this, and I found it frustrating, particularly when I first returned to Earth after our initial meeting. I'd have preferred to be told which steps I needed to take to move forward, and the best and easiest way I could integrate everything I'd learned with him in the spiritual realm into my life.

I wanted to know what to do when I was faced with other challenging situations in my life, and I didn't understand why he wouldn't give me any more answers, even though he was so close to me. I found myself feeling disappointed when he'd say, time and time again: 'You can do whatever you want, Anke. Just go with your gut and then decide. Everything is open to you.'

This wasn't what I wanted to hear, because I was still petrified about making my own decisions. I behaved like a little child who looks up to their father and constantly asks him what they should do, willingly and gratefully placing the responsibility into his hands.

The Power of Choice

Only much later did I fully comprehend the meaning behind my teacher's behavior and the great gift it held. He made me grow up internally and brought me into my power. He made me see my own potential and taught me the power of choice. This is how I eventually shed my anxiety around decision-making and realized that there's no such thing as a right or wrong decision. And that's the meaning of life – it's all about growing up and taking responsibility.

I remember one evening sitting at my son's bedside listening to him talk. He was going through a tough time because there were decisions to be made that he didn't feel ready to make. 'Tell me what to do, Mama,' he begged.

I smiled at him and said: 'I'm your life's witness, my love. I'll always be with you, and I'll always have your back, but it's not my job to make decisions for you – you're perfectly capable of doing that on your own.

'All the solutions you're looking for already exist in this field of infinite possibilities. It's your choice and only you can decide what you want to do. Create your own experiences and find out for yourself what works for you and what doesn't. There's nothing wrong with making mistakes, and there are no wrong paths to take.

'Everything that you choose, no matter what it is, allows you to gain valuable experience; otherwise you wouldn't make that choice – trust me. I'll always be there, even if you stumble or fall. I'll be there when you find your path and I'll celebrate every win. But it's up to you now to grow up and learn to trust yourself. I promise that I'll never interfere with your choices. I'll always respect them, and I'll only intervene if you find yourself in real danger. If that happens, I'll be there to catch you.'

I think I remember this conversation so well because I was surprised at the words that fell from my mouth. They came of their own accord and were so strongly borne of unconditional love that they left no question unanswered. In the same loving way, I feel supported and loved by my great friend, my nameless teacher.

CHAPTER 7

A New Perspective

I can't say exactly how long my near-death experience lasted. It could have been seconds, but to me it felt like years because I was given such a vast amount of information, knowledge, and experience – enough to last me 10 lifetimes.

While I was in the coma, my body was monitored by machines that kept it breathing and constantly checked its condition. Tubes supplied it with food and fluids, and now and then it received some love and attention from visitors. Not from me, though. Two days after my burned and broken body had been admitted to the hospital and I'd moved further away from it than ever before, something happened that confused me enormously.

Abruptly and without warning, I was torn from the suspended state in which I felt so wonderfully free and unencumbered, and brutally catapulted back into myself. I fought against it with everything I had, but it was hopeless. In an instant I felt my body's heaviness and almost unbearable burden once more.

The realization that I'd returned felt like a punch in the stomach. Shocked, I tried to cry out, but no sound came from my mouth. I was so stunned by this dramatic change in my situation that when I think about it today it still takes my breath away. I desperately tried to expand my consciousness once more, to get out, but nothing worked. It was as if I'd been bound and gagged, and was trapped in my own body.

After I'd calmed down a little, I attempted to get my bearings. The first thing I noticed was that I was no longer lying in my soft bed in the intensive care unit but was being lifted rather roughly onto a cold, hard metal table by two men. I found out later that this was when I was given a tracheotomy, a procedure in which the trachea (windpipe) is opened and a breathing tube is inserted so the patient can breathe without the use of the nose or mouth.

A Cruel Reunion

'Hey, could you be a bit gentler?' I grumbled. It reminded me of when I'd first arrived at the hospital, only now I was inside my body and I could no longer watch it from the outside and wander around the room in that wonderfully detached way. It appeared that we were to be reunited for good, my body and my consciousness.

My eyes were shut tight, but I could see right through them. Two doctors in surgical gowns and caps were present, and a young nurse was assisting them in their work. She had medium-length dark-blonde hair, was very petite, and seemed to be the only person in the room who was concerned if I was OK.

With the utmost care, she covered me with green sheets and arranged surgical instruments on a small table next to my head. Gently, she placed a pillow and some cloths under my neck and carefully adjusted the position of my head so that my neck was exposed. As she disinfected my neck area, I could smell her subtle perfume and feel her warm smile. No matter what this nurse did, she seemed to sense my presence and she gave me her undivided attention.

In my mind, I heard her talking to me: 'Everything will be all right. What we're doing here is important and it will help you to breathe better. Don't worry, the doctor is the best we have, even if he is a bit gruff sometimes. He knows exactly what he's doing. You're in good hands.' I wish I could have given her a hug because I was truly grateful to her, and what she said reassured me immensely. She must have sensed my fear because it seemed the most natural thing in the world for her to talk to me.

I've undergone quite a few operations in my life, and I've never felt afraid, but this one will stay in my memory forever. Not because I was in such great pain, but because I was completely aware of everything that was happening, even though my body was unable to move or make a sound. I felt the doctor's fingers on my neck as he made the small incision. I could read his thoughts, which were mechanical and highly focused on every step of the procedure. Unlike the young nurse, however, he had no idea that I was there – well, that I was conscious – and treated my body like an inanimate object. To him, I was just another coma patient who needed his help.

And what *didn't* I thought-shout at him as he roughly shoved a tube down my windpipe! 'Hey, I'm not a piece of meat! Could you do that a bit slower? Hello, excuse me... stop ignoring me! I can feel that, and it hurts! You can do that when I'm dead, but not now.'

While the doctor was busy with the procedure, his lovely assistant stood by my side the entire time, stroking my arm. She spoke to me constantly, although her lips never moved. She kept encouraging me to persevere, telling me that everything was going to be fine, and that she was looking after me.

Unfortunately, I can't remember the nurse's name and I didn't see her again, but I'll never forget her. For some reason, she could tell I was there, that I was conscious, and that I could hear her. I drew such strength from this young woman, who continued to find exactly the right words to help me overcome my fear. Even now, I can feel her touch on my arm and hear her reassuring voice.

Shortly after the tracheotomy, I was gone again. Exhausted, I returned to the warm embrace of my teacher.

The Body Holds Its Own Universe

Oh my God, that had been *terrible*. I *never* wanted to go back into that body again, nor to experience the unspeakable cruelty of being at the mercy of life. It took me a while to feel my teacher's love again because the shock of what I'd experienced ran deep. It threw me completely off balance and reminded me of everything I'd been through – the narrow confines of my life, my depression, my despair. So abruptly, that had become my reality once more.

The worst part was that I'd been unable to control that body, to communicate with it. I'd been unable to use my mouth to speak or to move my muscles, and yet I was fully aware of everything that was happening to me. Something was being done to me that I couldn't resist or oppose, and I'd felt utterly powerless and helpless. However, as I'd later find out, the procedure had proved invaluable for my recovery.

Naturally, I found I had a lot of questions for my teacher: 'What was *that*?' I asked. 'It was dreadful. Why did I feel so constricted in my body? Why did I feel so powerless? It felt like the heaviest burden, the exact opposite of the way I feel now that I'm with you again. Here, I'm vibration, expansion, and space. I'm lightness, limitlessness, and love. I'm everything I want to be. But being in my body felt so horribly tight and heavy.'

'Your body isn't a prison, Anke,' he explained. 'Your body has its own consciousness, and it has stored memories of everything you've experienced in your life so far. It also stores every thought and feeling so that you always have access to them.'

To emphasize his words, my teacher brought me to the elevated perspective I'd come to know so well. But this time, the energy felt much denser and more compact somehow. As he so often did when he wanted to make me aware of an important connection, he allowed me to look at my life from the perspective of a neutral observer.

I noticed quickly that I seemed to be particularly in tune with my thoughts and emotions. Although I *saw* the pictures that my teacher wanted to show me, first and foremost I *felt* my feelings in each situation, and I *knew* what I was thinking.

I learned that my physical body holds its own universe – one made up of an infinite number of fine energetic structures that are constantly changing. In this living ocean of energy, I could dive into every part of my body and explore its subtle vibration. From my organs to my blood and lymphatic circulation, right down to the vibration of my cells, everything seemed to consist of very similar expanses to those in the universe – only denser. This realization radically changed my perception of my body, and I'd like to make a comparison that illustrates this.

Multidimensional Perception

We owe our visual spatial ability to the fact that we have two eyes. Each eye perceives an object from slightly different perspectives, and our brain then calculates an image using depth effect. As a result, we see the world around us in three dimensions. Our other senses allow us to hear sounds, smell odors, and feel movement, and our brain combines all this sensory information into what we experience as perception.

Now, if we want to make a movie, we point a camera at an object and focus on it to record what's happening. If we shift the focus slightly so that the background is less sharp, the filmed object stands out more and attracts our attention. However, if we then add a second camera and film the same object from two different perspectives, and record sounds coming from several different directions, the result is the 3D effect we're familiar with from TV and cinema screens. A second, parallel, perspective gives our eyes a much more realistic visual experience.

This is the world as we understand it with our senses, and our brain processes it all for us. However, if we now imagine that we have five or even 10 cameras pointed at the object, we're getting closer to the heightened, multidimensional perspective I experienced in the spiritual realm. And if the cameras were not only able to record all these different perspectives but also all the feelings, thoughts, and contexts that are vital for truly setting a scene, we might have something like a 7D cinematic experience.

The Search for Meaning

Theoretically, this kind of perception is possible for humans, but what prevents us from achieving it is our limited beliefs and preconceived ideas about reality. As I've mentioned, in my heightened state of consciousness – detached from my body – I was able to grasp the most complex connections, down to the smallest detail, all in a moment. If, for example, I asked about the formation of the universe, multidimensional images would appear instantaneously, revealing everything there was to know about it.

I recognized my soul's almost endless field of consciousness; I understood the substance and focus of every single aspect of it and in so doing was able to experience myself as part of the whole. No matter which area I focused my attention on, the moment I did so I was able to see and understand *all* the connections, not only visually but also through knowledge.

This explains why so many people who have had a near-death experience report such different elements to it. Even though there are similarities – including the experience of unconditional love, which is revealed to almost everyone – each person pays attention to what's most important to them personally and therefore only receives answers about those things. For example, I wasn't concerned with reuniting with relatives who had passed into the spiritual realm. No member of my immediate family had died, so it wasn't surprising that no one came to greet me. My personal interest was almost exclusively focused on the meaning of life, the meaning of my experience in a human body, and the meaning behind our separation from the spiritual realm.

When I reflected on this, I realized it was this very search for meaning that had led to my accident and thus to me receiving answers to all my questions in this wonderful way. My near-death experience allowed me to gain a new perspective on my life – one that's left a lasting impression on me.

A Field of Light and a Dark Cocoon

My teacher then steered me in a new direction, stretching my multidimensional perception further still. As I'd done before, I was able to watch my life like a movie that I could rewind and fast-forward whenever I wanted, but now, my attention was not only drawn to the various experiences I'd had, and how and to what extent my body reacted to them, I could also see my ethereal being. My view from these two different perspectives – one physical, one spiritual – made me even more aware of the connections I'd come to recognize and understand so well.

Once again, I was able to see myself immediately after my birth, struggling to take my first breath by myself and surrounded by a radiant field of light. I'd been ejected from the protection of my mother's womb and found myself on a cold, hard surface. I was overwhelmed by the harsh lighting, the loud voices filling my tiny ears, and the huge hands that poked and prodded my body. It's no wonder that my very first experience on planet Earth was stored in my cells. 'Go away! Leave me alone, all of you! I can do it by myself!' was the first decision I ever made, and it was to shape the rest of my life.

I was born in Frankfurt in 1968 during a time of great upheaval and restructuring in Germany. My father was a young medical student at the time, and my mother was the most loving mother

I could have chosen. Growing up, I was a bright, friendly child and still fully connected to my spiritual home. My brain was like a sponge; I eagerly absorbed everything I saw because, somehow, I already knew that this would be very important for me in the future. When I think about the anticipation I felt and my curiosity about this adventure on which I was embarking, I'm filled with a great love for my younger self.

Now, as my teacher showed me the first years of my life, I had to laugh as I saw little Anke, with her limitless thirst for knowledge, wanting to try out everything and anything. She was so open to new things, and at the same time she had the gift of intuition, knowing exactly what was good for her and what she needed.

Disconnecting from the Source

However, as the years passed, the openness with which my life had begun faded, and I saw how, unconsciously, I'd maneuvered myself from one dead end to the next. What I was witnessing no longer had much to do with lightness. I saw how my fear and self-doubt had grown steadily until I became completely isolated. It seemed that loneliness and overwhelm had replaced my natural lightness. As I watched all this, I thought: *Why did the way I think about myself change so drastically? Where did my openness, my light, and my connection to my soul go?*

In response to these questions, my teacher drew my attention to a thick, dark cocoon which had formed around the radiant field of light that had been present at my birth. He told me that it was responsible for my disconnection from the Source, my spiritual home, and my True Self. In the training that followed, he showed me how, over the course of my life, this cocoon had gradually been getting denser, separating me from the higher levels of my soul. (I'll tell you more about the formation of the cocoon and its purpose in Chapters 12 and 16.)

I observed that the more I aligned my thoughts and actions with the ideas and rules of those around me – that is, my parents and teachers – the thicker the cocoon became. The more I conformed, the more I lost sight of myself and the thicker the cocoon became. I was speechless, but also fascinated. It suddenly made sense that I'd always felt so isolated and alone.

My teacher showed me how I'd become my own worst enemy and harshest critic. No matter what I did, nothing was good enough for me, and as a 'reward' I punished myself with feelings of guilt. The more my original essence – who I really am – was diluted, the more I lost sight of what fulfilled me. I adapted, subordinated myself, and began to hide from everything I was afraid of.

I watched as the various stages of my life played out, fast-forwarding and rewinding at will to relive a situation and fully immerse myself in it. As I did so, certain milestones – those where I'd made important decisions – became clearer. And when I saw the consequences of these decisions, all the alternative outcomes also appeared, and I was shown what would have been had I made a different choice.

I realized that for me, life had never been about fame, fortune, or familial bliss; all the things that we humans often wish for so fervently wouldn't have given my existence greater meaning. I could see all the paths I'd taken, as well as those I hadn't; I could see where my talents lay, see my learning steps, and why it was that I'd strayed so far from who I really am.

Losing Myself

When I looked at the little heap of misery I'd become, I was filled with the deepest compassion. Was that really me? How could I have been so cruel, so relentlessly harsh with myself? How could I have broken my own spirit so callously? I'd been so busy trying to please other people that inevitably I'd lost myself in the process. Far too often, I'd judged myself for my own words or actions. I'd forgotten to trust my intuition and instead I'd sought to control everything inside me. I'd struggled to find a kind word for myself, instead criticizing everything I did.

> *If you knew what a wonderful, abundant being*
> *you are, you could never be unkind to yourself.*

My eyes had been opened to how much my life had been impacted by my fear of condemnation and rebuke. Everything I did, I did only to be loved; to be recognized. I'd always believed that I was fighting for love on the outside, but the real battle was internal, taking place deep inside me.

I saw, too, that my body had taken on an important role in all this. Every negative thought and every destructive feeling had been stored in my cells all these years. My body had borne witness to my life. Every self-reprimand and criticism had accumulated in certain parts of my body, and now there were areas where the pain of past experiences ran so deep that it appeared as large, dark stones.

My body carried the loneliness, fear, and resistance I'd experienced throughout my life. I understood now why it had felt so terribly heavy and tight when I was squeezed back into it during my tracheotomy. I'll go into more detail about my changed perspective of my body in Chapter 11.

Waking Up

During the review of my life, I saw that one thing has remained constant throughout my life: the radiant field of light that was present at my birth. While it's changed in intensity, the light has been within me every second and it's always there, waiting.

If only I'd seen my field of light, I could have accessed everything that would have reminded me of my true nature. The finest threads of light emanated from it, countless in number and extending in all directions. They connected me to everything that existed, and they also formed an unbreakable link to my spiritual home. *Everything* was there.

In the simplest terms, here's what I'd learned from my spiritual teacher by this point. We humans *are* unconditional love; however, we then we embark on a journey, throughout which we completely forget this and become separated from the Source, our true home – only to rediscover it within ourselves through our feelings and thoughts. In other words, the meaning of life is to fully experience this unconditional love for ourselves and our environment.

Any difficulty, pain, and destruction we experience in life is always the result of becoming disconnected from the Source and our True Self. There's no other reason. But as soon as we begin to wake up from our deep sleep, various doors start to open. We start to move in the right direction, and we gradually remember our original essence. No matter how far we've strayed from ourselves, we all eventually wake up. Even if it's only in the moment of our death.

CHAPTER 8

The Field of Infinite Possibilities

The part of my experience in the spiritual realm that I've just described made a profound impression on me, leaving me feeling both dismayed and incredibly moved. I couldn't believe how harshly I'd judged myself and how unloving I'd been. But at the same time, I was filled with admiration for the courage I'd shown in plunging headfirst into the human experience. Truly, I could have made it so much easier for myself.

However, this new perspective on my life also brought with it more and different questions. So far, I'd learned to better understand my feelings, recognized my radiant field of light, felt the dark cocoon around me and the heaviness of my body, and seen and interpreted the connections between the events of my life. But was any of it *real*?

Everything that my teacher had presented to me so tangibly had been the reality of my life just a few days earlier. Before the fire, I'd tried to escape my unbearable inner emptiness by going jogging, and I was angry with God because I blamed him for my condition. Now, I found myself in a state of all-encompassing, unconditional love. I felt completely fulfilled, my limitless consciousness able to grasp everything I turned my attention to. *That* was also real, but there were worlds between those two experiences.

I took these thoughts to my teacher and asked him: 'Who am I *really*? Am I what you've just shown me, or am I what I'm experiencing myself to be right now? It just doesn't add up.'

'Everything is equally true,' came his calm reply. But from the vibration of his words, I also sensed a degree of anticipation. Once again, he seemed to know exactly what my questions were all about, and which training was appropriate for me.

'What you think is reality isn't reality. You define reality as something static, tangible, and fixed, but nothing is static, tangible, and fixed because everything – and I mean everything – is subject to constant change,' he explained.

'There's also more than one reality because what each person considers real is determined by their personal point of view. Reality is only an expression of how you see things. Do you understand? I'd much rather explain illusion and reality to you because that's what this is about.'

Playing with Reality

It's difficult for me to describe what happened after this exchange – as I've said before, human language isn't designed to convey such extensive ideas – but I'll try to bring you close to the magic of the experience and give you a sense of what it was like.

Until that point, I'd been so busy taking in everything my teacher was explaining to me that I'd barely paid any attention to him and his golden-yellow energy field. But then, for the first time, he showed himself to me in a human body. I can't remember exactly what he looked like because everything faded away when I noticed the way he looked at me.

Never had I gazed into such loving eyes; they made me feel as if they knew me inside out. Whole worlds were reflected in them – they were like a gateway to the universe and far beyond. With great astonishment I observed how, with only a slight movement of his hand, my teacher had changed his shape completely. A little boy stood before me, grinning at me mischievously and with an air of defiance. He was barefoot and wearing shorts with blue braces and a loose white shirt. 'This is reality,' he said.

My surprise at his abrupt transformation seemed to delight my teacher, but he didn't make any effort to provide an explanation for it. Instead, he winked, clicked his fingers, and instantly we found ourselves in a dreamlike garden. 'This is also reality,' he beamed. Countless flowers and plants of a kind I'd never seen before bloomed around us, and there was a beguiling scent in the air that almost made me dizzy.

No sooner had I begun to take all this in when my teacher snapped his fingers again, transporting me to another 'reality.' This time, instead of him, a beautiful woman stood before me – although the word 'beautiful' barely begins to describe her. She wore a long dress bathed in light with a delicate golden belt. Countless sparkling diamonds formed each strand of her long, golden-blonde hair. But the most striking thing about her was the huge diamond on her forehead, which shimmered in all colors.

The woman's warm-hearted gaze expressed everything that we humans try to put a name to using terms like love, wisdom, and truth. All of this was united in her. 'Let me show you reality,' I heard her say as our surroundings transformed once more. We were now on a snowy mountain top.

'These are all reality, Anke. Reality is a creative process that's continually drawing on itself and creating itself anew in each moment. This continuous re-creation is a playful, curious, and wholly conscious process,' the woman explained as she changed our surroundings once more with a gentle hand movement.

Still speechless and awestruck, I watched her transform not only her own appearance, but that of everything else, using only her thoughts. The realities in our environment began to change, this time moving faster and faster. Like in a time-lapse film, landscapes moved and reshaped, and my teacher's figure changed constantly along with them – he showed himself to me as Jesus, the Buddha, a Native American chief, and a bear.

The Creator of My Own Life

Again and again, my teacher took on the most diverse forms and colors, in between becoming pure consciousness without adopting any form. It was all exactly the way he wanted it to be in any given moment – and it clearly gave him great pleasure.

'You can do it too,' he smiled at me affirmatively as he transformed our surroundings into a lively summer meadow. 'I could explain a great many things about this process, but it wouldn't really help you. You must experience it yourself to understand it. Give it a go! What would you like to create or what form would you like to take? Just make your choice and see what happens.'

I remember my first, very clumsy, attempts very well. In my frame of mind at the time, I didn't believe that reality was changeable, so what my teacher had just shown me was simply miraculous. Even so, I was astonished when suddenly, a small, beautifully formed Christmas tree stood before us. It was the first thing that had come to my mind, and I still laugh heartily when I think back to that moment.

A Christmas tree – how on earth had I come up with that? But this was about being creative, not clever. My teacher still shows me this little green Christmas tree sometimes when we talk about this topic. I only had to think of a Christmas tree and there it was. It was as real to me there in the spiritual realm as my teacher was.

I quickly realized that everything I was thinking about was taking shape before me, becoming tangible and completely real. It was pure magic – and a lot of fun. One after the other, a multicolored umbrella, a streetlamp, a pond with a rowboat, and every animal imaginable all appeared. Laughing delightedly, I snapped my fingers at each new idea that sprung into my mind, feeling like a little child excitedly discovering the world around me. I soon learned that I could make the Sun bigger or smaller; I could make it snow and then turn the snowflakes into gold sparks. Whether I concentrated on just one thing or on transforming everything I'd created at once, the only thing that mattered was my idea and my intention. I learned to change my own form, too. I could become a tree, a deer, and the breathtakingly beautiful woman my teacher had appeared to me as earlier.

'I think you get it now,' my teacher laughed, after letting me practice for a while. 'You create your own reality with your thoughts. It all depends on your perspective and where you focus your attention. Do you understand?'

Yes, I did understand, and how! He'd shown me in such a light, funny, and playful way that it was solely up to me how I shaped my life. I was feeling very enthusiastic about this wonderful experience and would have happily gone on like this forever, but he gently stopped me in my tracks.

'Do you *really* understand the extent of all this?' There was a note of urgency in his voice. 'You're not being graded on this, remember. It doesn't matter what you create for yourself – you're not limited by anything of your own choosing. You can create whatever you want, and that means you can automatically *achieve* it too.

'It works the same way with feelings, experiences, or situations. It was you who created the confines of your life – the heaviness and the pressure – and that's what became your reality. You are the creator of your own life.'

Reflecting on My Experience

Every single thought that we have creates something. With every thought, we build and create all the things on which we focus our attention. We're the creators of our own life. Every thought sets a process in motion, and this makes us highly creative because, after all, we have an infinite number of possibilities at our disposal at any given time.

In every moment of our lives, we make important – or unimportant – decisions with our thoughts. We decide what to eat, what to wear, how to react to certain situations, or whether to do something or not. We decide whether we want to change an unpleasant situation or keep it the same.

> *Your life is a creative mirror of your own perspective. Change your perspective and your life will adapt to it.*

From a spiritual point of view, we create or change the reality of our lives in every moment, and we can also redesign our lives at any time. We can always choose to decide *for* ourselves or *against* ourselves, to choose conflict or peace, to choose a difficult path or an easy one. But this power of choice, this field of infinite possibilities, is something that we're usually unaware of.

I certainly wasn't aware of it before my near-death experience. I knew that I could change things in my life, but my fear of this very change was stronger. I was so convinced that I wasn't lovable enough, good enough, or strong enough that I decided I'd prefer to leave things as they were. Instead, I focused my attention almost exclusively on my problems. I busied myself with areas of my life that I found difficult and restrictive.

And today, I can see it was inevitable that my life would become increasingly difficult. After all, I'd created it myself. For years, without knowing it, I'd created limitations, darkness, and fear. I'd brought these things into my own life, and they had become my reality. The more attention I paid to them, the more clearly these qualities were expressed in my life.

If I'd known back then what I could achieve with my thoughts, I'd have been much more careful and attentive about what I was thinking. What I witnessed in such a wonderfully playful way with my teacher has now changed my life completely and enriched it enormously. Now, I consciously tap into the field of infinite possibilities. My fear, and my self-sabotage, have vanished, and my teacher's assertion that 'everything is possible – everything is already there!' is my lived reality.

The Gift of Amnesia

I'd like to tell you the story of a man who came to me for counseling a few years ago because it fits so well with what we've been talking about. He was 45 years old and had led a successful, albeit very stressful, life. During his childhood, life had dealt him a bad hand – he'd lost both his parents in a car accident and had grown up in a children's home – but as an adult he'd worked his way up to a management position in a large company and was responsible for 4,000 employees.

When I met this man, he was living with his wife and their two adorable children in a posh suburb of the German city of Hamburg. However, a few months earlier, his life had changed radically overnight when an accident caused him to lose his memory. He couldn't remember his past or what he did for a living; he didn't know his name and he didn't recognize his wife and children. Everything he'd experienced before the accident was what he described as a 'grey nothing.' He no longer knew what fulfilled him because all his memories had disappeared in one fell swoop.

Interestingly, though, he seemed to view this situation quite positively. He told me in detail about what he and his family had tried to do together to recover his lost memories. His wife and children had spoken to him for hours about what had been important to him before the accident – what he liked to eat, the things he liked to do. They took him to certain places, went into work with him on several occasions, and invited friends over to their house.

But none of this brought back the man's memories. Everything his family told him felt alien to him and none of it mattered – he felt as if they were talking about a total stranger. He'd heard about my accident and was hoping I could help him fill in the blanks. He saw his situation as a chance to find out what he *really* wanted in life.

I worked with the man for a few months; we spoke on the phone once a week and I told him a lot about what had happened during and after my near-death experience, and how I've viewed and lived my life since. He began to figure out for himself what sparked joy in him and what made him feel good. He said he felt as if he was standing in front of a large buffet, overwhelmed by all the unfamiliar dishes because he couldn't remember what any of them tasted like or even if he'd tried them before.

He attempted everything that came into his head and as a result, got to know himself on a deeper level. He also explored a lot of the things he'd been told had been important to him prior to the accident, but it turned out that he didn't like or enjoy most of them. There was nothing for him to sort out; he had nothing old to let go of and could instead play around until he found out what he wanted to spend his life doing.

Today, five years later, he's one of the happiest people I know. He has a pilot's license and is currently training to become a professional pilot. He and his wife have taken the opportunity to fall in love with each other all over again, and spending time with his children brings him the greatest joy. The family now own a dog and they've moved to a cozy house by the Baltic Sea. This man's transformation made quite an impression on the people who knew him before his accident, many of whom began to question and change things in their own lives, too.

Why am I telling you this story? Because it conveys so beautifully what life is about for us. However, what makes me sad is the fact that we humans tend to undergo such transformations only when there's literally no other way. For some reason, we're terrified of change, and it's only when tragedy strikes, or we experience a great loss, illness, or some other wake-up call, that we're finally ready to lean in to what truly makes us happy. We start to question what we're doing, how we're living, and what we really want, until we're able to make long-overdue decisions and begin to consciously shape our existence and live it in the way we want to.

Chapter 9

The Source

A gentle yet determined current pulled me higher and higher; it felt like an embrace, enveloping me, and allowing me to expand further than ever before. I was filled with an indescribable feeling of bliss and surrounded by beautiful and impressive sounds, colors, and vibrations. The sounds were limitless and pervasive, like the song of heaven, and I sensed I could almost reach out and touch them. It was as if all the consciousnesses of Creation had gathered here to welcome me.

I truly felt that Creation had been revealed to me in the form of sound, color, and vibration – that in this wonderful way, I'd been incorporated into everything it holds. This cosmic melody was inescapable – it was in me and all around me – and what's more, I *was* this sound and all sounds at once, as well as every color and every frequency. I felt my own consciousness merge with this all-encompassing symphony.

Myriad colors emerged before my eyes, and every sound I heard brought me to a new dimension. Together, this incredible chorus and the endless colors danced the dance of Creation, inviting me to fully immerse myself, to connect with it. It was the most beautiful and fulfilling thing I've ever experienced. It felt as if I was right at the center of the Source, from which everything originates and into which everything returns. I felt it pulling me in, so I could call its universal wisdom back into my own consciousness.

Oh, how I'd have loved to stay there, but I knew that I couldn't. No matter how hard I tried, I couldn't control anything that was happening to me in the spiritual realm. If I'd been able to, I'd have watched this breathtaking, melodious spectacle in slow motion, so that I could savor every moment, down to the tiniest detail.

The Cosmic Symphony of Creation

As I observed everything that was happening around me, I noticed some of the swirls of color begin to open, like gateways into other worlds. Suddenly, I found myself looking at planet Earth, which didn't appear to me physically but instead as an enormous, creative, living field of consciousness. Within this mass of frequencies and vibrations, I could perceive a wide variety of qualities, which the Earth seemed to unite as one. The planet exuded both feminine and masculine energy at the same time.

To me, the Earth felt like the kind of mother who loves all her children equally and who gives them the space they need to live out their own experiences. I'd never been able to perceive our world, which I'd previously experienced as heavy and dark, in this incredible way. Every person, every soul to whom it provided a home, was connected to the Earth, and simultaneously to the cosmic Source, via innumerable threads of light.

Absolutely everything was permeated by the cosmic symphony of the Source. What I'd previously considered evil, bad, or tragic simply ceased to exist, no matter where I looked. Everything was imbued with an indescribable sense of unconditionality, as if to offer up space for infinite potential experiences in various possible worlds.

Suddenly, the color spectrum that moments earlier had given me this breathtaking view of the Earth changed; the sounds and notes shifted slightly, and I watched the planet fall away from me. Another gateway had opened, and now I found myself immersed in a completely different realm. Planets flew toward me, along with solar systems and whole galaxies, filled with all kinds of life. World after world opened before my eyes, and all were connected to the Source in a way that felt completely natural.

Nothing escaped the sound. Nothing fell outside the unavoidable reach of its symphony. I found myself wondering how I could ever have felt so alone, so disconnected, and as if my life had no meaning. There were so many worlds, so many dimensions, and all were part of a spectacular tapestry of color and sound! Every solar system, every galaxy, and everything else I saw had its own consciousness, its own field of vibration. I could see nothing, anywhere, that wasn't anchored in this consciousness.

I saw dimensions and worlds that seemed to vibrate at far higher and much more subtle frequencies than those of our planet, and they were home to far more intelligent life forms.

Reflecting on My Experience

By this point in my journey the information I'd been given wasn't knowledge as we humans would define it. It's not something that can be understood with reason; there are no facts that I can explain, and no tangible proof of anything. Even now, I can still barely get my head around it all. What was imparted to me in the spiritual realm can only be described as 'pure knowledge' and it far exceeds my limited understanding of it. But at the same time, it feels as if everything I saw back then has been forever ingrained in my memory, my own inner world, on another level of reality.

In the years since, it's become clear to me that all the vibrational planes that are home to humans are multifaceted and connected with all the other worlds out there. Every consciousness is a rainbow of colors and incredibly creative in its own way. We're all part of an infinite cosmic play of experiences and an all-embracing process of creation.

We live here on planet Earth in the most diverse cultures, follow the most diverse beliefs, and are subject to the most diverse influences. We all carry our own personal truth within us and experience our own reality. And yet we all come from the same Source. We're all permeated by its spectrum of colors and sounds and are inseparably connected to it.

Creation's Indifference

The Source is unconditional. It has no concept of right or wrong, good or evil, yes or no. For the Source, everything is equivalent, and this means that we can always tap into its abundance. The Source is indifferent to the way we live, although this indifference should not be equated with irrelevance.

Good deeds and bad deeds are the same thing to the Source because nothing *means* anything. These are human definitions that don't exist for the Source. For the Source, everything that happens is of equal value, of equal meaning, and serves solely and exclusively to help us create ourselves anew.

> *The Source wants us to recognize ourselves as*
> *our own creator, to have our own experiences,*
> *and to learn and grow from them.*

It wants us to make creative choices and to get to know the implications of those choices, no matter what they are. It makes no difference whether we're suffering or happy, because the Source isn't keeping score.

Nothing means anything, and yet all the painful experiences we successfully navigate our way through do in fact have great meaning. These experiences cause us psychological distress, and it's precisely this internal suffering that pushes us to change something. Remember: Everything you're looking for is already within you.

The 'pure knowledge' I received on my spiritual journey feels like a pulsating force that I can still access today and with which I feel fully connected. I can still remember everything I learned, even the tiniest detail, and I continue to re-immerse myself in the spiritual realm because none of it seems to fade.

Now that I'm back in my body, however, I'm bound by its laws and I've noticed how much my mind looks for tangible concepts to make sense of the world around me, concepts that simply don't exist. When I write, I'm always struck by how my cells react to the high vibrations I'm trying to explain to you; the cells themselves vibrate at much higher frequencies than usual and it feels like they're trying to express all the colors and sounds of the Source through my body.

I have to withdraw gently from the memory of my experience so I can continue to concentrate on the words. The higher level of consciousness in which I found myself during this stage of my near-death experience has since become a natural part of my being, as if it had never been otherwise. There's no more separation; everything is one.

As I write, my body is showing me how connected it is to everything I'm telling you, and it's also responding to my thoughts. I feel the consciousness of my cells without having to leave my body or switch off my mind through meditation. This is one of the greatest gifts I brought back to Earth with me.

You Must Remember!

I used to think that the kind of experience I had during my coma was completely impossible, or perhaps only accessible to a few select masters. Today, however, I believe that it's entirely possible for humans to gain conscious access to the higher spiritual realms with the help of our innate abilities – and that it's also possible for us to realize them within ourselves if we want to.

We've carried the tools for this within us since time immemorial. We can direct our attention through our consciousness; we can stop dwelling on what we think we don't yet have; and we can turn our focus to the adventure of self-discovery. As soon as we manage to set aside the thinking and permanently judging mind and are ready to let ourselves fall into the higher vibrational dimensions, whole worlds open. This much I know, and I'll talk about it more in Chapter 17.

At their center, the body's cells have direct access to the Source, and they are the key to directly experiencing Creation through the body.

> *Knowledge about our origins, and the fact*
> *that we're connected to everything that*
> *exists, is anchored in each of us. Always.*

I'm not special; I've not been chosen, and I didn't earn any of these insights through anything I've done. The vibration of the Source is anchored in you just as it is in me, and you also carry this knowledge within you like a golden treasure. Deep in the center of each of your cells, you're aware of this. And each of your cells wants nothing more than to be allowed to express this vibration, this sound. That's exactly why you're here. We don't have to die to have this experience.

Prior to my accident, I'd heard others say that we're all divine, that we're all a part of God and that He loves us immeasurably. But at the time, this just felt like empty words to me. I heard them, but they made me feel sad because I couldn't feel any truth in them. Nothing in *me* felt divine – quite the opposite, in fact: nothing in me felt loved.

Today, these words are my reality and they've become a code for my life. On my journey not only did I gain knowledge about all the connections in my life, but I also anchored myself in the state I was in at that time – for eternity. It's for this very reason that I'm not only aware of the truth of these words, but I also feel this connectedness within me and try to live it as best I can. I no longer have to seek things out because I've found everything that I need within me. I no longer have to look outside myself for things I think I lack because everything I truly am is anchored within me.

This has become an unconditional truth for me. And it's precisely this truth that I speak to inwardly when feelings of sadness or separation arise in me. Whenever I feel down, I gently lean in to the feeling and embrace it, just as my teacher did with me. I acknowledge this wounded part of me, and I realize that all these feelings could only have arisen because it felt separated from the Source. Lovingly, I whisper to it: 'You must remember! I'm going to show you who you are.'

CHAPTER 10

The Dance of the Gold Dots

As I stood amid the cosmic symphony of the Source, a whirlpool of vibration, sound, and color drew me into its center once again. It was like a current that was gently but steadily absorbing me, pulling me deeper and deeper – a current that captured everything it touched and united it.

The sounds, colors, and vibrations that surrounded me consolidated and seemed to become more present, somehow – like a great choir into which new voices constantly flowed, making it sound louder and more powerful, filling the room. This cosmic whirlpool drew me in at full intensity until, suddenly, the center of the Source catapulted me into a completely new experience of being.

Here, in stark contrast to the liveliness of the Source, it was utterly dark and peaceful. I sensed a powerful, all-embracing emptiness and absolute silence. As if I'd been blown up and scattered far and wide into countless fragments of consciousness, in this dark, peaceful nothingness I was suddenly everything and nothing all at once.

My sense of self dissolved, and all that remained was an eternal presence. To my amazement, I *became* the dark, peaceful nothingness. It was overwhelming. There was no longer the 'me' who was on an exciting journey, the 'me' who wanted to acquire knowledge and for whom experiences were so important. I learned that everything that's born and dies is a manifestation of this eternal, absolute presence – me included.

Arriving Home

This abrupt change to a new environment came as a surprise and although I tried to orientate myself, it was impossible to do so. Floating, at rest within myself but at the same time completely dispersed, I became aware that everything I'd been shown so far and everything I'd ever experienced as a human being or as a soul had the sole aim of leading me right here – into this limitless space of peace.

It was as if I'd become a moment of eternity, and all previous knowledge and experience lost its meaning. Nothing felt important to me anymore; nothing caught my attention. Now that I'm trying to tell you about it, I'm finding myself immersed in this fulfilling peace once more, and I feel as if I could conclude the book right here. It's a state that needs no description because it already contains everything.

When we're immersed in this creative space of peace, everything else loses its meaning and our consciousness slips into a seemingly endless eternity. How I'd love to bring you here to me in this state so you can experience it, too. Can you even imagine it? Maybe you can feel it, or maybe you already know it.

This all-embracing peace into which I'd dissolved contained everything I've ever experienced; I'd arrived at everything that is. I felt that it contained the deepest essence of my being, my original nature; I felt as if it were the primary Source that we sink back into after a long, long journey.

Soon, I heard my teacher's voice again. 'Where do you think you are?' His words came from everywhere at once; they even seemed to emanate from within me, like a gentle breeze.

'I've... I've arrived. I'm home. Nothing is more beautiful and fulfilling than this,' I whispered back. I heard his warm, loving laugh and I knew that he too was a part of this indescribable peace.

Cosmic Tickling

Feeling as if I was slowly waking from a restful sleep, I suddenly realized that there were dots of the warmest, brightest gold shining all around me. One after another they appeared, multiplying rapidly. Big and small dots of warm golden light that seemed to be alive flashed out of the darkness, exuding a joyful liveliness. They appeared to radiate from within themselves and were constantly sharing, as if they wanted to fill the entire space with their happiness.

As I tuned in to these fascinating gold dots of light, I felt their power and their desire to expand. They looked as if they were engaging in a playful dance, full of enthusiasm about their pure existence and ready for anything. The dark and peaceful space was transformed into a vibrant, happy, and abundant one. I couldn't help but laugh as I watched them play because their liveliness felt like a cosmic tickle. Never had I experienced something so light and playful yet powerful.

The more I laughed and engaged with their dance, the more radiant the dots became. I realized that they and I were miraculously connected through our consciousnesses, which made me feel so excited and alive. They wanted to show me everything they could do; it felt like we were inspiring each other.

These dots of warm golden light seemed to exist on a different level of reality to the Source, but at the same time they didn't. As I experimented with my attention, I realized I could look at each level of reality separately by adjusting my focus, as if I were observing nanoparticles through a high-resolution microscope. I could see the Source itself as if I'd penetrated a subatomic reality, but I could also focus only on the dance of the gold dots.

I then noticed that the dots, which were vibrating at an incredibly fast speed, were each in the center of a much larger, wafer-thin sphere. Curious, I focused my consciousness on the spheres, and suddenly more and more of them appeared before my eyes, all filled with an infinite number of cheerfully vibrating gold dots.

The spheres reacted to me in a way that was very similar to how the dots did. When I felt love, they became brighter and bigger and radiated out of themselves. But if I remained neutral and watched their vibrant, joyful dance without intention or emotion, then their vibration remained the same.

The Vibration of Eternity in Our Cells

'What are all these wonderful spheres of light and dots that are making me laugh so much?' I asked my teacher. 'A moment ago, I was anchored in a peace that felt like the source of Creation, and now I'm dancing with sparkly gold dots. Where am I?'

'I'll show you where you are,' I heard my teacher say, as I was drawn away. It felt as if I was in a whirlpool again, and although it was as gentle as before, this time it was pulling me downward at great speed. Suddenly, I found myself back in the intensive care unit at the hospital, standing with my teacher alongside the bed where my motionless body lay. I recoiled in horror. That couldn't *possibly* be me – I was barely recognizable.

Since I'd last seen it, my body had become extremely bloated and the severe burns on my face, neck, and hands had all undergone extensive and complex surgery. The doctors had taken skin from my thighs and grafted it onto my hands, and a cell culture transplantation – a method commonly used to treat extensive burns – had been carried out on both the destroyed and partially charred skin on my face and neck. Both hands and my entire head were wrapped in thick white bandages and countless tubes ran to a machine that beeped monotonously. I'll never forget the sight of this mummy-like body.

My teacher seemed to sense my alarm and in a gentle, calming voice he told me, 'Everything possible is being done to support your body, but the most important thing is still missing. The doctors have helped it, but what it really needs is you!'

'I don't understand! What am I doing here?' I cried. I looked at him pleadingly. 'I really don't want anything to do with this body! Why would it need me? Please take me back to the tickly gold dots.'

Using no words but with an intensity that frightened me, my teacher did exactly the opposite. Without waiting for my consent or giving me the slightest chance to resist, he dragged me relentlessly back into my body. He led me through the layers of injured skin into the tissue underneath and showed me dark, deeply traumatised areas. I was aghast. Not because I was particularly perturbed by the injuries, but rather because it brought me back to the terrible experience I'd had during the tracheotomy.

I fought against what my teacher was doing with everything in me. For the first time since I'd met him, familiar feelings of defiance, rebellion, and even anger – against everything and everyone – arose in me. He was speaking to me, but his voice was distant and even his golden-yellow energy field felt constricting. A flood of sadness came over me and I suddenly felt very lonely.

'Pay close attention and trust me,' he whispered in my ear and this time his voice was clear. I was relieved to have access to him again, despite my emotional chaos.

OK, you win – I admit defeat, I thought, finally succumbing to what was happening.

On the journey through my body, I saw various organs, glands, and bones. I was pulled deeper and deeper into the tissue, right down to my cells. 'Pay close attention, Anke, and you'll realize once more that nothing exists separately,' my teacher said.

As I flowed into one of my cells, I suddenly understood what he wanted to show me and why it was so important. My resistance quickly turned to enthusiasm as I penetrated deeper into the cell, layer by layer, and recognized the vibration of eternity at its center. Here, I also found the continuously multiplying gold dots again – a welcome discovery, given that I'd just been so abruptly pulled away from them.

My teacher's words affirmed what I already knew within myself: 'Yes, you've arrived. You've arrived and are at home within yourself.'

Reflecting on My Experience

I used to think my body was irrelevant. It served me to get from A to B and to communicate with other people, but if I'm honest, I didn't particularly like it, and I whined and moaned at it all the time. Looking back, I think that my body even scared me a little because I knew I was dependent on it. I wouldn't have been able to exist without it – or so I believed.

My biggest problem was that I didn't know my body and therefore I didn't really trust it. I couldn't control it; it could have developed a disease or any number of other issues at any time if it wanted to. If our car breaks down, we take it to the garage, and if it's so badly damaged that it can't be repaired, we buy a new one or take the bus. Unfortunately, it's not that easy when it comes to our bodies. Conventional and alternative medicine research the body and try to understand it, the Church considers it sinful, and we ourselves mostly ignore it.

However, the truth about everything that we are is stored in the body. We can ignore this truth, but it cannot be changed. Everything we put into it – every thought, every feeling, and every rejection – is stored there. This is exactly what I experienced when my teacher forced me to engage with my body: I felt the familiar emotions of fear, anger, and sadness, and I barely felt connected to it anymore.

If we want to become whole, to really connect with ourselves, there's no getting around the body. For it's much more than a vehicle that makes our existence possible. It offers us the space to create our own experiences and we alone are responsible for it.

The body is Creation personified.
Creation turned into matter.

Our bodies are a limitless field of consciousness in which every single cell acts on our thoughts and feelings. If we punish our bodies with ignorance or rejection, they will patiently absorb everything until eventually, their stores will overflow. As a last resort, the body will *force* us to address it; it will find a way to show us what it wants us to do. Guaranteed.

Listening to My Body

When I was suddenly freed from my body by the accident, I had no desire to go back to it under any circumstances. Today, though, I'm very humble and truly grateful for my body. This change happened a few years ago and it was the biggest turning point in my life, my greatest awakening; I talk about this more in the Rebirth and Renewal section.

Now I live in my body, and I truly and completely respect and love it. I've recognized it as a golden key that enables me to experience true fulfilment. It hears my every word, reacts to my every feeling, and we've developed a new, common language that we use to communicate. Our language is one of mutual loving care, and we understand each other in a way that wasn't possible before.

Since we've been paying attention to each other in this way, I've experienced joie de vivre through and with my body. I love my life and myself in a whole new, wonderful way, and every cell in my body celebrates with me.

I can promise you something very important at this point: No matter what your body is telling you right now, everything can change as soon as you start to love yourself. Your body is just waiting for you to do it. The day comes for us all when the body ceases to function, but you'll continue to exist even when your body dies; you'll move on and experience yourself in a completely new yet very familiar way.

CHAPTER 11

Humankind's
Greatest Treasure

During our visits to my body in its hospital bed in the intensive care unit my teacher often watched me silently and observed my reactions. So far, I'd found the experience rather unpleasant, and I didn't fully comprehend why he was taking me there. It was still crystal clear to me that I'd never return to the heavy shell of my body, even after I'd been shown its connection to the Source. We were worlds apart now.

The sense of freedom and limitlessness I had in the spiritual realm, and the state of unconditional love, were so fulfilling that I'd have been more than happy to leave the unconsciousness of my life behind forever. On the next visit, however, I felt much less resistance toward my body; in fact, I had a gentle sense of recognition.

For the first time in my life, I could really *feel* my body. I felt what it felt, and I was connected to it in a whole new way – one that was almost loving. Suddenly I was able to communicate with its consciousness. Was this possible because my teacher had allowed me to engage with my body when I'd traveled to the center of its cells? I felt its sadness and despair that I'd turned my back on it so radically.

The more I felt my body, the more I became aware of an obvious truth that had escaped my notice until then. I'd believed that I was trapped in my body, that I was dependent on it, but in fact the opposite was true – it was dependent on me. I was the one who was free and limitless, and I was the one who could expand into the spiritual realm, not my body. Without me, it would cease to exist.

I, on the other hand, didn't need my body at all. I understood that its existence would lose all meaning if I continued to reject it, because I was its only point of reference. It was only here because of me. This entirely new perspective triggered real appreciation in me for my body for the very first time.

The Body, Our Sacred Vessel

Stunned, I turned to my teacher for guidance, and he approached me with a smile. Until now, he'd mostly stayed in the background when it came to my body, but now he stood next to me, giving me the serious, piercing look he used when he wanted to tell me something particularly important.

'This body is a sacred vessel formed especially for you,' he told me. 'As I've told you before, it possesses its own consciousness, and this is in no way tight and rigid, as you previously thought. Instead, it consists of a vibrational signature that's perfect for you.

'Your body is changeable and fully connected to the Source, even if, right now, you don't think that's possible. Your body is your vessel, Anke. It's the greatest treasure a human being can behold, and it bears the key to absolute fulfilment!'

'But in my experience, my body *hasn't* been a key to fulfilment,' I grumbled, feeling a little ashamed. 'For me, life in my body was the opposite of fulfilling.' I couldn't quite grasp the meaning of his words, or maybe I just didn't want to. I remembered the many times throughout my life when I'd treated myself very unkindly. I'd somehow forgotten how to feel and view myself with love.

As I spoke, scenarios in which I'd experienced unhappiness, loneliness, and inner emptiness appeared before me, and I realized that the more often these states arose, the tighter and heavier my body became. I felt sad. If I'd paid more attention to my own needs and wishes, it would never have come to this. If only I'd given myself the same love I felt for my children and my husband, none of this would have happened.

Love, this natural, God-given state, was what I'd always longed for. I *could* feel love, but I felt it for my family, for my friends, or for the environment – never for myself. And this was exactly why I didn't want to go back to my life: I'd simply moved too far away from myself.

My Pre-Planned Wake-Up Call

'Have you ever wondered why I'm showing you all this?' my teacher asked. 'Why I made you aware of the connections in your life, led you to the Source and back to your body time and again?' This question surprised me, but he was right. Throughout everything and all the wonderful things he'd shown me, I'd never asked myself why. He'd shown me that he'd always been by my side, throughout all my lives and all my births and deaths. The idea that our encounters could have another meaning hadn't occurred to me.

'Your physical death was never the issue during our journey together, Anke,' he explained kindly but seriously. 'We made an agreement, a long, long time ago, and we've now honored that agreement. You carefully planned the accident with the fire, so it could serve as a valuable opportunity for you to consciously leave your body for a longer period. This was necessary for you to be able to fully experience your True Self, the Source, and your consciousness.

'Everything that we've experienced together was scheduled by you before you were born. You decided on this comprehensive training, no one else. It was important that you perceive yourself. Can you still remember? That's exactly what happened.'

By then, I'd experienced enough and had been through sufficient training to recognize the truth in my teacher's words. I *had* decided on the details of this life in advance, including the specifics of my death and the nameless teacher who would bring me to the spiritual realm. I'd scheduled a wake-up call, a safety net, for the middle of this life, and I knew exactly why: I wanted to make sure that I remembered my True Self and integrated it into myself. I remembered it all!

I'd planned to express the qualities of my soul in my body; to truly inhabit my body with all the higher planes of my soul. I wanted to find out whether it was possible for me to activate my soul with the help of my body – to bring it to life through my consciousness to express unconditional love. This was the daring and courageous adventure I'd pre-planned for myself in this life.

And I'm beyond grateful for this wake-up call, for my accident, because without it I'd never have realized to this extent all the miracles and possibilities that are available to us as human beings. Instead, I'd have been swallowed whole by feelings of helplessness and powerlessness.

A Life-and-Death Decision

In the same moment, I also realized why I'd always felt as if my body was waiting for something: It was waiting for me to decide whether I'd reconnect with it or break away from it for good. Its entire existence depended on this one decision. By now, all of this had become clear, yet the idea of returning to my body and having to continue living within its confines still didn't feel very appealing.

'Do you mean to tell me that it's up to me whether I choose to live?' I asked my teacher. My look of surprise seemed to amuse him. 'Do I even have a choice?' I continued. 'Can I decide for myself?'

'Yes, of course you have a choice! It's entirely up to you – it's your decision what happens next,' he replied. 'No matter what you choose, it will always be the optimal choice for you. Remember that there's no right and wrong. You're not bound to anything, and you can change everything at any time. You can amend every past decision, alter every feeling, and turn your attention to completely new areas at any moment if you want to. You've already had enough practice with me.

'These same possibilities exist for your body, too. You can change everything if you're willing to engage with your body. However, if you decide to reject your body now, it will no longer be at your disposal. Your conscious decision to accept or reject your sacred vessel is of the utmost importance, so take your time! This decision holds a golden key.'

Every word my teacher spoke left a deep impression on me. For added emphasis, he brought us both to the elevated observer's perspective we'd adopted so many times. I watched as our journey together unfolded before me, condensing all my experiences and knowledge, and making them clear once again. I knew that I myself had set out all the challenges I'd faced in my life. I'd been in control of everything that had happened to me – my entire life had followed an elaborate plan, *my* plan.

My teacher told me once again about the spiritual connection with my family and with him, and how I was always and forever connected with everything I'd so desperately sought, reminding me of the unconditional love that connects everything that exists. He showed me once more the field of infinite possibilities, the Source of which I'm an indelible part, and the ever-multiplying sparks of gold that dance in each of my cells.

Everything happened simultaneously and mysteriously, and this time my body's consciousness seemed to be involved as well. What I'd previously experienced as I'd been detached from my physical body now seemed to happen in it or with it. My body had access to the spiritual realm, and it had always been able to access it; I just hadn't realized it.

Reflecting on My Experience

Our physical body possesses an intelligence that reaches beyond the human mind. Forgive me if I'm repeating myself, but I really can't emphasize this enough. When you consciously see and, above all, *experience* the spiritual areas of your body, you make contact with vibrations that feel quite miraculous.

The body is truly a colorful, rich, and vibrant energy field that permanently resonates and communicates with its surroundings and our consciousness. The way I see it, it's made of the finest light structures, and the space in and around its cells is pure liveliness and joy. It loves to vibrate and to react to vibrations, transforming them into color and sound. It's a constant, lively pulse that can renew itself independently and adapt to new circumstances.

The body's mission is for us to experience life in it and through it. It's directly connected to the Source through its cells and DNA.

However, the body responds solely to our individual human consciousness. It's like the biggest and most incredible high-performance computer imaginable, but it can only be controlled by the one person it was created for – you.

Unfortunately, we humans struggle to truly perceive this finely vibrating, energetic miracle, and we usually only notice it when it shows us that there's a disturbance in the system. As the Buddha said, the human body holds all the teachings, all the suffering, the cause of suffering and the end of suffering.

We *wanted* to be born into the body we inhabit, and we each chose a body that's perfect for our needs. Whether we're aware of our body or not, and whether we like it or not, it doesn't change anything – it expresses exactly what we need for our own growth and the process of self-awareness. When the body's ill, the illness has a deeper meaning for us; if we feel that the body's restrictive, if we reject it or fight against it, this also has a deeper meaning – *our* meaning.

I've worked with countless people over the years, some of whom were very unhappy or felt very challenged physically. All these people were fighting against themselves, and their body tended to reflect this struggle for survival. But it was a struggle that they could end by deciding to take a closer look at themselves and learn the language of life and the body.

They'd all distanced themselves from their True Self and, through fear, had split off large parts of themselves. Over the course of their life, they'd struggled to access their higher level of consciousness. They'd inhabited their body with only a fraction of their True Self, and, just as I'd done earlier in my life, they'd barely engaged with it.

Most of them had feelings of hurt, anger, guilt, or fear and had successfully learned to suppress them. Unfortunately, we humans are masters at that. However, as I said earlier, the body stores our life story, and it's of little use to us to repress our own history. If we do so, it'll be the body that tells us our story one day, in its very own way. It will lovingly but ruthlessly force us to open the doors we've closed on ourselves.

CHAPTER 12

Expanded Consciousness

Everything I discovered and experienced on my journey to the spiritual realm has its own consciousness. My teacher has his own field of consciousness, my body has a consciousness that I learned to communicate with, and my cells have their own consciousness, just as planet Earth and Creation have their own consciousness. Our consciousness connects us to the consciousness of everything around us and things far beyond, and these fields of consciousness only differ from each other in their vibration, frequency, and focus.

For our consciousness, concepts like 'above' and 'below,' 'inside' and 'outside' don't exist. At the onset of my journey, I'd felt myself being drawn 'upward,' but was that really what happened? Maybe I'd just wanted to escape the situation at the hospital when I first met my teacher and therefore assumed he was pulling me 'up.' I'd always thought that God, salvation, or the universe were outside of me – maybe that was the reason.

Today, however, I know that there's no such thing as 'up' or 'down.' Nothing is outside of us because we're connected to everything through our consciousness, and our consciousness has no limitations. All the limitations that we experience are created solely by our thoughts, and because our thoughts are bound to space and time and cannot otherwise orientate themselves, they create limits. In moving beyond these limits, we can expand our consciousness into limitless*ness*.

> *Everything you think you know about yourself*
> *is only a drop in the ocean of your True Self.*

Throughout my near-death experience I visited countless different fields of Creation, each of which revealed to me their unique insights, impressions, and focal points. These unknown worlds felt so alien and were mainly revealed to me through images, although some consisted only of sounds and frequencies. As soon as I'd consciously experienced one of these realms, even once, I only had to think of it to find myself back there.

I could move between all the wonderful fields my teacher had guided me into as often as I liked. All I had to do was think about the Source and I'd find myself back in its essence, and a single thought about my teacher was enough to bring me back to him. My consciousness had expanded into these realms, and I was now able to enter them simply by thinking about them, whenever and however I wanted to. And this worked whether my consciousness was in my body or outside of it.

The Cocoon of Consciousness

Obviously, all the wonderful realms of Creation had been there before I'd experienced them, but I'd never thought to look for them. In my reality, they simply hadn't existed. I had no idea of the real possibilities available to me and to what I was connected.

Before the accident, I'd focused almost exclusively on my problems, spending most of my time thinking about feelings and situations that I found unpleasant or uncomfortable. I'd been looking for a solution to my life situation and in so doing I'd failed to realize that my *point of view* was the reason why nothing ever changed.

It was only when my teacher taught me to expand my consciousness into the fields of Creation, to really experience them, that I realized that unconditional, spiritual love was my true nature. I just hadn't been aware of it. The Source, my teacher, and the limitless love I experienced myself as a part of, had always been deeply anchored in me, but I'd never focused my attention on it.

While I was talking to my teacher about this realization, he drew my attention to something we'd discussed before, during our review of my life. I saw that when I was a few months old, a change had taken place in my radiant field of light: it was enveloped by a fine veil. With my teacher's help, I put myself in the place of this veil, and I immediately understood more about its purpose: it had made me forget where I came from.

It had drawn my attention inward – to myself, my body, and my human needs.

My teacher explained that it was only with the help of the veil, which can also be thought of as our ego, or our thinking mind, that I could perceive myself as an independent, individual human being and get a true feel for myself. I'd been able to focus mainly on my body and experience my own needs through the veil. Without it, I'd have continued to feel connected to my spiritual nature and unconditional love.

He also showed me that this fine veil had become thicker and thicker throughout the course of my life and the sum of my experiences, until eventually it became a dense, impenetrable cocoon that almost completely limited my consciousness. This was why, in more recent years, I'd felt so isolated and alone. Metaphorically speaking, I was stuck, trapped, inside this cocoon. Perhaps you understand how this feels and have experienced what it's like to run up against your own internal walls.

The Illusion of Separation

I suddenly saw the meaning I'd been searching for all my life: We're not separate, we haven't lost anything, and nothing has been taken from us. We're still connected to our spiritual home. No matter how we feel, we're fully connected to the Source and are never separate from it.

We're all infinitely great and powerful beings; we need only to snap our fingers and everything we want becomes possible. No power that we know of is equal to our own limitless energy and creative power.

> *We have the potential within us*
> *to create everything we desire.*
> *Abundance is our natural state.*

We know no lack; we love to be creative and express ourselves in the most diverse ways. As infinitely creative, wise, and unconditionally loving beings, we have the limitless desire to give free rein to our creativity and to delight in our own creations.

It's only because we're inside our cocoon – which to us seems impassable – that we think we're separate from the Source. But that's an illusion. The cocoon is like a snow globe, a sealed-off world that we believe is our reality. We've forgotten that we're so much more than that; I'll talk more about my teacher's snow globe analogy in Chapter 16.

I'd never have been able to live a life of extremes if this cocoon hadn't formed around me. It wouldn't have been possible for me to feel lonely, isolated, sad, or worthless because I'd always have remained aware of my connection to the Source and everything that exists. This was the most important step toward realizing the fulfilment and self-love that I experience as my reality today. Within me, not outside myself.

Everything Happens for a Reason

We sleepwalk through life because we've forgotten what we've planned for it, what experiences we want to have, and what we need in order to have those experiences. We've forgotten that everything is available to us, that we have access to everything we need to make this possible.

But this forgetting serves a purpose. We're here to have experiences and therefore it would be counterproductive if we knew we had a magic wand we could wave to change everything about our lives in any given moment. Being as clever as we are, as soon as things became disagreeable, or difficult, or dangerous, we'd wave our wand, realign a few thoughts, and reshape things however we saw fit.

We'd never know pain, or discomfort, or poverty, or failure because we'd know how quickly we could change or improve our situation or condition. And we'd rarely experience sadness, fear, or loneliness, because those aren't pleasant feelings. We'd also behave very differently if we were loved unconditionally. We'd stop being so hard on ourselves. We'd never feel anger for another person, let alone want to harm them. We'd love every other human being and ourselves unconditionally because we'd recognize every creature as the beautiful, finely vibrating being that they truly are.

So, from a spiritual point of view, it's not about living a perfectly easy life as a human being, because if it were easy, there would be nothing for us to grow and learn from. We need to experience the limits. We need figure out what those limits are and then find a way to break them. So, there's a good reason why we've forgotten everything that's available to us and why we don't always get everything we want.

Finding Our Purpose

We are here on Earth to experience the full effect of our separation from the spiritual realm, from our True Self, and its associated isolation. This is exactly why we chose our physical body (we can only enter the illusion of time and space through a physical body; the body is what makes it possible for us to experience ourselves within duality as 'separate' from everything else.)

It's part of our life plan to be a unique, separate individual and to forget our true spiritual home and our True Self. The cocoon that settles around us is indispensable for our adventurous journey. It allows us to experience life as a series of challenges and to learn to master those challenges in our own way.

We're not here to fall victim to life, even if it often feels that way. We're here to learn to love ourselves – regardless of our circumstances.

Many things that seem problematic or negative at first glance offer great opportunities that often turn out to be the most valuable gifts in life. They can teach us how to change our perspective and go in search of ourselves. Crises sometimes force change on us, but it's up to us to recognize the meaning behind them and to make our own decisions.

Inevitably, we'll all reach a point when we can no longer fool ourselves into thinking we're alone. We're part of everything, part of the bigger picture, no matter how much we turn a blind eye to it; ignoring this fact only keeps us feeling small and stuck. In truth, the more difficult life becomes, the louder the wake-up call and the chance to remind ourselves of our True Self.

As soon as we look up and acknowledge the miracle that we are, we're sure to find our way back home – to ourselves. We don't need to look for love outside ourselves, nor do we need a redeemer or a god to free us from our eternal suffering. We are the only ones who can redeem ourselves.

Remember the drop of blood I told you about in Chapter 6? That drop of blood stands for you, and it holds everything you think you know about yourself; everything that your current 'me' perceives in this world. Our ego is in this drop of blood. In other words, everything we perceive as our reality within our cocoon. Everything we believe about ourselves is in many ways essential for our conscious development, but it can also be destructive.

Only our ego allows us to experience ourselves as a human being in a human body with a unique personality. Our ego helps us to individualize ourselves, but it can only do so if it first separates us from our True Being. And this is how we get lost in the illusion of separation. But as soon as the inner, conscious changes begin, we remember our True Being and come home to ourselves. We break away and drip back into the sea we came from.

CHAPTER 13

My Unconditional 'Yes' to Life

Many people who have a near-death experience or who suddenly perceive themselves outside their body because of an accident, return to their body just as quickly as they left it. This usually happens without conscious intention and without warning. They often describe their return as like waking up from a dream, one in which they gained a brief insight into the nature of reality that never quite fades away.

I've also heard of people who had specific reasons from a spiritual perspective for their return. Just as I did, many had to choose whether to return to life or not. Often, deceased family members informed them of the consequences of their decision, and sometimes they were even sent back with a clear mission if they still had something important to take care of. For many of these people this seemed like the most difficult decision imaginable, but soon it became the easiest of all.

As I've explained, I experienced a return to my body when I was forced back into it without warning during my tracheotomy, and the shock ran very deep. No one wants to go back to a cramped, dark prison from which they'd escaped. In addition, my body no longer looked particularly attractive, so in all honesty, I had to think very carefully about what I wanted to do.

'It's about truly inhabiting your body,' my teacher told me several times when I questioned him about the monumental decision I had to make. When I think back to those conversations today, I smile, because I now have the greatest understanding of my inner turmoil at that time.

A big part of me wanted to dive back into the adventure of life as quickly as possible, to joyfully put into practice all the wonderful insights I'd gained during my journey. This part of me felt fully awakened, fulfilled, and connected to everything. It was aware that there was no separation and that I could only have experienced what I had in the past because I'd forgotten who I really was and where I came from.

But there was another part of me that was so terribly afraid to take this step. It didn't yet trust my body and it was petrified of diving into unconsciousness again and having to live in inner emptiness and loneliness once more. This part of me also didn't feel ready for the challenge of living in a disfigured body. I felt terribly torn between these two sides of myself, and the easiest option would have been to listen to the loud 'no return' I felt inside me.

Reconnection

Today, as I reflect on those moments as I write this book, I feel grateful that my great teacher wasn't impressed by my reluctance to return to my body and that he took it seriously. To help me decide, he showed me how the soul returns or leaves the body during pregnancy and at the moment of death.

Almost as if it needs to get used to the universe within its tiny body, the soul gently slips in and out of the tiny fetus, tentatively at first, and then gradually more often. Similarly, when the hour of death approaches, the person's consciousness slips out of the body, pays longer visits to the spiritual realm and then flows back into the body. Leaving or returning to the body is rarely abrupt or traumatic.

My teacher made me aware that I had a wonderful and unique opportunity here if I approached my body just as cautiously, but also consciously. I could gently engage with it, get to know it, and in the process find out whether I felt comfortable with it. This suggestion really made me sit up and take notice because this way, the anxious part of me could gradually determine, at its own pace, whether it wanted to go back.

I'll never forget the special moment when I began to reconnect with my battered body. At first, it took an incredible amount of effort, as I was firm in my belief that it was tight, rigid, and heavily burdened. But my fear of losing the connections or the experience of oneness when I returned from the spiritual to the physical world was even greater. In the event, I was proved wrong on both counts.

After some deliberation, I finally let myself go very slowly and carefully back into my body. Immediately, I noticed that nothing had changed – I continued to be in my awakened state of full connection. The more I engaged with my body, the more I could feel its joy. Its anatomy felt anything but tight and heavy – quite the opposite, in fact. Everything was so vivid and flowing; it was like an explosion of vibrations and frequencies. Everything was subject to an order that I can only describe as all-encompassing.

I let myself go deeper and became increasingly aware that my body seemed to lead me in its very own way. It communicated with me by showing me its infinite energy pathways, light structures, and color vibrations. It was as if I'd been allowed to enter a magical, breathtakingly vibrant wonderland for the first time, one where I never ceased to be amazed. My body's spiritual and earthly planes seemed to merge smoothly, and I could switch between them at will. I could identify very bright, highly vibrating areas, but I could also dive into darker, almost tough-looking planes that seemed to be completely bound by the laws of physical reality.

Making Friends with My Body

My fear gave way to amazement at this very special world I'd entered, and the more I opened myself up to it, the more I could feel its joyful vitality. Like an old friend who had finally found me again after a long time apart, my body took me by the hand, beaming, and showed me its universe. It took me into its organs, into the skin and the bloodstream, and let me experience their respective vibrations and functions. I realized how lonely and unseen it had felt without me and how happy it was to be consciously connected to me once more.

How had I been able to inhabit this body so blindly? How could I have so shamefully neglected and ignored this miracle of my own creation? Meanwhile, the apprehension I'd felt about my body's physical matter had given way to bright enthusiasm, and this only increased, becoming the purest anticipation of living my life in this indescribably vibrant body-field of frequencies. I wanted to experience what it means to live in harmony with my body, to keep communicating with it, and to accept it completely.

My teacher had insinuated often that humans lack conscious connection to the body and that this is the cause of illness or negative feelings. We're so far away from experiencing perfect health and fulfilment and this is because we've forgotten that we come from the Source and are eternally connected to it. We don't need to do anything more than remember that. As soon as we enter our natural state of light vibration and fully accept our bodies with our consciousness, everything that vibrates at a lower frequency than our own light resonates with it and is transformed.

The Mission

In my excitement about the breathtaking worlds that I'd just discovered within myself, I'd completely forgotten everything else that was happening. My consciousness was so intimately connected to my body that I'd blocked out the space around me and my teacher, as well as the very important decision at hand. I felt the love of my teacher flow through me as he gently directed my attention toward him.

'I see you've already made a decision,' he said kindly, placing his right hand on my head, which was wrapped in thick bandages. 'You once came into this body and forgot your connection to me and to yourself. Now that you've returned, you've remembered, you've entered your very own spiritual world, and you're once again aware of your True Self and your connectedness. All of this, my love, will remain unchanged. Once you've attained self-awareness, it's no longer possible to descend into unconsciousness.

'Don't be afraid. Go back, learn to love yourself, and live a fulfilled life. Your mission is to express the unconditional love of your soul through your body. It carries everything you need for a conscious and fulfilled life. Really bring it alive with your love for yourself, and as a result, experience the miracles you're capable of achieving together. You'll find a way to use this power within yourself and in the world around you to support other people on their journey. Everyone carries the memory of their True Self within them.

'I'd like to tell you something very important about your upcoming journey. You should break your limits! Please, never forget that. Break your limits. Nothing happens by chance, and everything originates from an order that's merely become *disordered* in some way. Everything fits together with everything else. Matter is always changeable and never static. Don't forget that!

'Just as your consciousness always has a choice and is capable of transformation, so too is your physical body. It will remember and heal, just as you hope it will. It will follow your consciousness and fully realign and renew itself if you so desire. Your face, your hands, and even your psychological condition will change – with the help of your physical body, you'll find your very own way. Trust yourself and always be aware of the miracle of Creation. I'll always be by your side supporting you, as I always have done.'

His words were imprinted on every cell in my body as I felt myself slipping into a restful sleep. My life was about to begin for a second time. In absolute peace, deep within myself, I'd finally arrived in my very own body-universe, its heartbeat like a cosmic song.

PART III

Rebirth and Renewal

CHAPTER 14

Echoes

My transition from the spiritual world to the physical was glorious. Every now and then I'd gently open my eyes, only to immediately slip back into the realm I'd come to know so intimately. I felt like an unborn child in its mother's womb, feeling her heartbeat and enjoying occasional glimpses of the world into which it would soon be born.

The doctors had changed the dosage of my medication to end the coma and initiate the 'waking-up process.' However, when I opened my eyes for the first time, there was no one in the room except the old lady in the bed next to mine – a familiar scenario. As I lay wrapped in soft, warm blankets, the devices still beeping and whirring away, I *felt* myself. I was fully aware that I was back in my body, and that triggered an indescribable feeling of gratitude in me. Exhausted, but at the same time eternally fulfilled after my long, eventful journey, I'd returned to my body.

The Return

'We're bringing her back now,' my husband had been told over the phone earlier that morning. 'But it'll take several hours for her to become responsive, so it should be fine if you get here around noon.'

This news spread like wildfire around my family; they'd all visited me daily and often sat by my bedside for hours. Apparently, my son had tears of joy in his eyes when he learned that his mother was finally being brought out of the coma. He would have dropped everything to come and see me but, thank God, he was spared that ordeal for the first few days because he wouldn't have been able to cope with the sight of me.

The door opened quietly, and a nurse entered the room. When he saw that my eyes were open beneath the thick bandages, he smiled calmly and naturally, as if I'd just woken up from a short nap. 'Good morning, young lady! I'm glad you're awake,' he said softly. 'I must share this good news right away. Please wait a moment, I'll be right back.' He disappeared, only to return shortly afterward with two doctors.

Just as the nurse had, the doctors behaved as if it was the most natural thing in the world that I was lying in bed hooked up to machines and unable to move. Later, I learned how important it is to treat coma patients in this way; they often find it difficult to orientate themselves after waking up or struggle to remember why they'd been admitted to hospital in the first place. How wonderful that there are such compassionate people in the world!

One of the doctors gently removed a plaster from my throat and carefully pulled out the breathing tube, allowing me to breathe unaided for the first time in nine days. The first conscious breath I took was a wonderful gift, even though everything still felt kind of stuck together. Being able to fill my lungs with air on my own and breathe deeply was pure bliss. I felt like I'd just been born into this world from my mother's protective womb, as if I'd taken my very first breath and with it cried out a loud 'soul' yes to my new life.

Two Worlds Become One

Initially, I felt unbelievably weak and powerless. I was given food through a tube and after each feeding session I gratefully drifted off into a healing sleep. Inwardly, however, my cells were rejoicing. They were primed for regeneration and renewal, and I carried within me the certainty that they would get me through anything. All was perfect.

When I think back to those first few days after I came out of the coma, I feel so moved because I'd never been as happy as I was at that time; I felt such a peaceful, deep inner happiness. Thanks to the treatment I received, I had no physical pain, and I was able to switch back and forth between the Source and my waking consciousness easily and naturally, each time arriving a little more fully into my body. Two very different worlds had merged into a new, perceptible reality for me. I felt embedded in my body, cared for lovingly by my nurse and my family, who were allowed to visit me for a short period each day. However, as the risk of infection was extremely high, I was allowed only one visitor at a time, and they had to wear sterile clothing. Everyone else sat behind a large glass wall that separated my room from an adjoining one.

I lost count of the times I opened my eyes to find my mother or my husband sitting at my bedside. I can't describe how wonderful it was to look into my mother's bright, grateful eyes and to see my father through the glass wall. The spiritual bonds and love that we shared, which I'd been able to experience through my teacher, was so tangible that it overwhelmed me. I could feel my parents in every cell in my body and I felt deeply grateful that they were with me in this life.

'I'm so glad you're here. We have so much to catch up on... Everything will be different from now on,' were the first words I whispered to my mother, as tears of joy ran from my swollen eyes.

Back to Life

Those first few days were a wonderful but very intense experience for me. I felt so safe, warm, and protected as I enjoyed the round-the-clock attention of my lovely nurse. He was so calm and gentle, and he did everything in an admirably matter-of-fact way. He changed my bandages with the utmost care, made sure I was always lying comfortably, and regularly moisturized the damaged skin on my lips until I was able to drink unaided.

Initially, I wasn't really interested in what exactly had happened to me. I didn't ask how things were looking under the thick bandages on my face or hands, nor did I care about my future. The only thing that mattered to me was love. Before long, I was able to have lengthier conversations without falling into a deep sleep, and as soon as I could sit upright and the thick bandages around my head had been replaced by thinner ones, I started lecturing my nurse about love. I told him how important it was for him to be just as attentive to himself as he was to his patients. I urged him to live a full and happy life because happiness is the meaning of life.

Shortly before I was discharged from hospital, the nurse told me that whenever I started to tell him about what I'd experienced during the coma, a strange look came over me that demanded his undivided attention. Each time, he'd smiled patiently and listened to me with interest, and he really made me feel that he was taking me seriously, but later, I wasn't so sure because my hospital report stated: 'the patient developed brief reactive psychosis after decannulation [removal of the tracheostomy tube], but it has progressively improved.'

Brief reactive psychosis is a state of confusion and temporal and spatial disorientation that often occurs after a patient comes out of a long coma. But I didn't feel confused or disorientated at all – quite the opposite! – although I admit I must have said some rather confusing things at times. In fact, I felt clearer and more present than ever before, and even though my poor body was still barely able to move, my mind, particularly my sense of self, was wide awake.

Eventually, I enquired about my condition and the doctors described in detail what had happened to me. They explained how they had treated the burns – some of which were severe – on my face, ears, neck, and hands, and how they intended to proceed with my treatment. But still, none of this really mattered to me. I knew with great certainty that my body would heal in a miraculous way and that it didn't need any help. Everything was perfect in a way I'd never experienced before, and nothing within me questioned that. Something had changed fundamentally, but I didn't yet know what it was. Somehow, nothing seemed to worry me anymore. I'd stopped thinking dark thoughts and had started feeling gratitude toward everything and anyone, including myself. This sense of certainty – that everything's fine the way it is – has stayed with me to this day.

Facing Up to My Face

Four days after I woke up from the coma, my nurse said to me with a smile, 'Today is a special day, Mrs. Evertz. I've heard that your son is coming to see you, and that you'll be allowed to get out of bed for the first time – if you feel ready for it. We could take you to the visitors' room in a wheelchair. What do you think?'

I was so happy when I heard this – the thought of seeing Manuel brought tears of joy to my eyes – but then doubt set in. 'Wait... how do I look? Will he be able to handle seeing me like this?' I asked the nurse cautiously. 'Please, I must know how I look before my son gets here. Do you have a mirror? I haven't seen one around here.'

'Yes, we do have a mirror. But first, I want to tell you something important,' he said kindly. Retrieving a small hand mirror from a cupboard he sat down with it at my bedside. 'I want you to know that you look great! We're all so pleased with how well you're healing. Your skin still needs a little more time, but....'

I didn't hear what the nurse said next because when I looked into the mirror he was holding up, I immediately burst into tears of shock. What on earth was *that*? The face staring back at me couldn't possibly be mine; this puffy, fleshy thing had no lips, no hair (the fire had claimed the eyebrows and eyelashes and any remaining head hair had been shaved off), and its eyes were bright red and swollen. What had once been facial skin was now red, raw flesh, some of which had formed dark scabs over the top. The only thing that looked even a little familiar was the nose.

For the first time since I'd woken up from the coma, I felt disheartened. Speechless, I looked at my nurse, who was gently stroking my arm. 'It looks a lot worse than it is,' he said, reassuringly. But I was barely listening. As I peered at my disfigured face again, my excitement about seeing my son gave way to pure fear; this creature looked nothing like his mother.

'No,' I mumbled defeatedly. 'Please call home and tell my family that I don't want to see Manuel. He won't be able to bear it. He can't ever see me like this!'

Tears streamed from my swollen eyes, and my inner lightness gave way to total helplessness. I felt as if I'd lost my identity. The positive way I'd felt about myself just moments earlier was now starkly contrasted with my horrific appearance. I found myself wishing I could just spend the next few months in the arms of my teacher.

The Best Medicine

'Now, don't be so pessimistic, young lady,' my nurse said insistently. 'Listen, the risk of infection is still very high, so we'll be dressing your wounds with a light bandage again. You'll also get a big mask and a fancy green bonnet for your head. I'm sure your son will be overjoyed to finally get to see his mama, won't he?'

Without waiting for me to object, he began to change my bandages, and an hour later I found myself sitting in a wheelchair, and feeling quite excited, in the visitors' room. Now I was the one wrapped from top to bottom in sterile surgical clothes, and the only things that were properly visible were my red-rimmed eyes. I'll never forget the moment the door opened and I saw my son for the first time since the accident. All my worries evaporated in an instant and I began to cry again, but this time with tears of indescribable joy.

The hour we were allowed to spend together was so therapeutic and the greatest incentive for my recovery. The whole time I just looked into Manuel's eyes, forgetting the surreal situation we were in. I laughed a lot and babbled on without pausing for breath. I can't remember what I said, but I talked a lot; it was as if a great dark wall inside me had simply collapsed. Manuel told me much later how difficult this first encounter had been for him. My family had tried to prepare him, though, so he'd had a rough idea of what I might look like beneath the bandages.

On the Road to Recovery

In the days that followed Manuel's visit, I recovered incredibly quickly and felt more and more alive as time went on. I felt a new sense of joy and a zest for life I'd never experienced before. The doctors removed my feeding tube, and other tubes and wires continued to disappear from my body. The huge open wounds on my face and hands were thoroughly cleaned and redressed with fresh bandages every day, and even my ears recovered well.

If my hands hadn't been rendered immobile by rigid splints and thick dressings, I'd have spent the whole day wrapping bandages or something else to keep myself busy. I was constantly pestering my nurses for something to do because I wanted to satisfy my desire for action. Although I wasn't yet allowed to, I tried to sit in the wheelchair next to my bed on my own, just so I could feel a little less restricted. I rolled it back and forth with my feet, but as soon as I was caught doing it, I was sent back to bed.

My joie de vivre and the renewal in my cells increased almost daily, and so it became increasingly torturous to be confined to bed. I wanted to run, to move, to get out of there as quickly as possible and go back to my old – yet completely new – life. I felt like I'd been resurrected and was capable of anything. There was so much I wanted to get to work on, so much that would change now, that increasingly I felt it was unnecessary for me to stay in the intensive care unit. I could recover just as well at home.

The principal physician, however, reacted quite sternly when I told him that. 'You're too euphoric,' he said to me more than once. 'I don't think you've actually grasped the seriousness of your situation yet.'

'The seriousness of my situation?' I responded. 'I just know what I need most right now, and I trust that!'

'You sustained severe burns and were in a coma for nine days, Mrs. Evertz. That's no laughing matter!' the doctor replied. 'Although we're very pleased with how well you've healed so far, your body needs time, and above all rest, so that it can recover from your ordeal. If you can't stand being in the ICU anymore, then perhaps we could consider moving you to a regular ward.

'Either way, you can expect to stay with us for a few more weeks. After that, we'll apply for rehabilitation with a chaperone for you. Due to the extensive transplantations on your face and hands, you'll also need to wear a face mask and gloves made of compression material for a longer period, so the tissue doesn't scar too much. We'll be able to correct a lot of things later with plastic surgery, when everything's healed, but that's going to take a long time.'

As I listened to all this, I felt the gentle vibration of my teacher at my side and heard his familiar words, which he'd conveyed to me so convincingly: 'Your body is so much more clever and powerful than you can imagine. Don't forget that! It will follow your consciousness and, if you let it, it will show you all the miracles it holds. Your face, your hands, and even your psychological condition will change – with the help of your physical body, you'll find your very own way. Trust yourself and always be aware of the miracle of Creation.'

Going Home

On 13 October 2009, 14 days after being admitted, I discharged myself from the hospital. I'd spent hours in talks with my doctors, who had tried everything they could to change my mind. It had been draining; I'd explained to them repeatedly that the only thing I needed now to recover was rest and the privacy and safety of my own home.

Naturally, they saw things differently, reeling off facts and empirical data and warning me of the risk of infection. However, my body stood firm in its decision. It knew what it needed, and I felt it strongly, too. I'd decided to trust my own inner voice, and it told me very clearly: *Go home. You don't need all this. You need protection and shelter to regain your strength and feel safe. Everything else, your body can do by itself. Trust it!*

My father is a naturopathic doctor, and I knew I'd be in the best hands with him, so even the principal physician's arguments couldn't change my mind, although he was visibly horrified by my decision. After an extensive session with a psychologist, who had been called in at short notice, I had to sign a four-page declaration that released the hospital from all consequences of my decision to discharge myself against the treating physician's advice.

Today, when I think about why no argument or facts would have convinced me to stay in hospital, I again feel this irrepressible need for love and security, both of which ranked far above reason for me. Nothing was more important to me at that point than being in a comfortable and familiar environment because I was doing so well for the first time in my life, even if I was the only one who knew it.

However, I must stress that my decision was incredibly out of the ordinary. It was an easy one for me to make because I felt that I had access to the best possible medical care from my father, but that doesn't mean that the doctors weren't correct to advise me against discharging myself and to outline all the potential risks that came with it.

Feeling exhausted but happy, I sat in the car as my husband made his way through the Munich traffic. Thanks to my teacher, I'd consciously made the decision to return to my body and to experience life through it, so we had a very special connection to each other. In fact, I felt that my body had taken the lead and I was just its mouthpiece.

CHAPTER 15

From Caterpillar
to Butterfly

I spent the first few days back home almost exclusively lying down – I slept a *lot*. Here, in my light-filled house, I felt safe and secure in my new reality. I wanted to be as close to my family as possible, so they made up a bed for me on the couch in the living room. As I lay there, my gaze fell directly onto the fireplace, but incredibly, the sight of it triggered a deep feeling of gratitude in me that I couldn't explain, even to myself. I can still see my son's puzzled face the first time I asked him to light the fire because I wanted to hear the flames crackling; but after that, he did it for me every evening.

Everything within me and around me felt so wonderfully new. I was in familiar surroundings, but I saw and experienced everything in a completely new way. Only two weeks had passed since my accident, but those two weeks had altered me, and my whole life, beyond recognition. Nothing was as it had been. I was forever changed.

I felt delightfully at peace, with a sense of having arrived home to myself that I can best describe as 'abundance.' I felt thoroughly fulfilled and could barely recall that agonizing inner emptiness that had characterized my life just a few weeks previously. I also experienced this same liberating calmness in my mind – the endless loop of negative thoughts had vanished, and I was no longer worried or fearful about the future.

Often, I just lay contentedly in my couch-bed, wrapped in soft blankets and happily listening to the lively chatter and laughter of my family. The memories of what had taken place during the nine days I was outside my body were present with astonishing clarity. Everything I'd experienced with my teacher in the spiritual realm filled me with indescribable gratitude and a blissful feeling of pure happiness.

Healing

The most beautiful thing about being home was that I was able to spend time with the people closest to me again. I owed all this to the wise foresight of my teacher, who had patiently encouraged me to re-engage with my body and my life. What a priceless gift!

I sensed that a large part of me was still living in the spiritual world because I didn't feel separate from it as I once had.

Concepts like 'here' and 'there' simply didn't exist anymore; there was no difference between 'body' and 'soul.' It was a state in which everything I was, everything within me, felt united and connected. I felt as if I'd returned to this life laden with spiritual gifts.

I took the medication the hospital had prescribed only on the first day, simply because my husband urged me to. I wasn't feeling much pain, apart from in the parts of my body where my bandages had been changed daily, so I didn't want to take the pills. My right hand, both ears, and parts of my face had suffered third-degree burns, which meant the tissue had been severely and irreversibly damaged. The tender, freshly transplanted skin was very oozy and had to be carefully looked after, especially on my hands. But removing the bandages, which stuck to my skin, was the only significant pain I experienced.

Overall, my skin healed incredibly quickly. We saw improvements on an almost daily basis, and I felt that my body was sending me a clear signal. Due to my thickly bandaged hands, which were still immobilized by splints, I required help with almost everything. I couldn't eat, take a shower, or change my clothes by myself. For every task I needed to complete, no matter how small, I learned to ask for help, and that was also a very new and healing experience for me.

God Doesn't Roll the Dice

Shortly after I returned home from the hospital, I was visited by a police officer who was investigating the accident. He'd already spoken to my family and put together a broad picture of what had happened, and now he wanted to hear my side of the story. Most of all, he wanted to see how I was doing.

'You've been incredibly lucky,' he remarked, visibly shocked by the extent of my injuries. 'I investigate many fire accidents, but yours is truly extraordinary. The flames from a bioethanol fire are merciless and practically impossible to put out. If your son had hesitated for even a second or made a different decision, we wouldn't be talking now.'

The policeman and I chatted for quite a while, and I told him in detail about my experience on the evening of 28 September. 'May I ask you how you can be so positive, and even smile, when you talk about your terrible accident?' he asked when I'd finished.

'Because God doesn't roll the dice,' I answered spontaneously. 'Everything in life happens in accordance with an invisible plan; nothing happens randomly or by chance. I'm smiling because there's nothing to be sad about.'

'You really are an amazing woman,' he replied. 'I feel incredibly moved by your story, in a way that I can't explain. I was also very impressed by your son when I spoke to him, and that's why I've sent my report to the district government and nominated him for the life-saving medal. I really think he deserves it.'

Manuel had overheard our conversation and had sat next to me on the couch when he heard what the lovely police officer said about him. He gave me a cautious kiss on my scabby forehead, grinning from ear to ear. 'I've got my mama back and that's all that matters,' he said. 'Besides, I don't think I did anything special or out of the ordinary.'

The medal was awarded to Manuel a few months later by the German chancellor during a special ceremony; along with a certificate, a watch, and a lengthy newspaper report, it lies at the bottom of a drawer in his bedroom.

The Stranger in the Mirror

The hospital had created a strict treatment regimen for me, one of the first steps of which was a stay of several weeks at a rehabilitation clinic for burns patients. I successfully managed to resist this, however, after looking at the facility's website and seeing that their primary focus was on psychological care and physical recovery. I didn't need either because I'd seen my body renew itself each day.

I often stood in front of a large window in our home, looking out at nature as it prepared for winter and admiring its beauty. I knew that everything was fine just the way it was, in every moment. Everything takes its time and follows a higher purpose. As long as I succumbed to this creative process, I'd be provided with all that I needed and everything that was important to me. The unconditional love I'd experienced in the spiritual realm was deeply anchored in me now and I was amazed to find out what that meant for me and my new life.

While I'd been given various salves to keep the skin on my hands and ears moist, it had been decided that open wound healing would be the best method for my face, which meant I didn't need any bandages there. My skin regenerated on its own under the thick, dark red scabs that had formed a natural protective layer. That was the only real challenge for me in the early days of my recovery. To get to the bathroom, I had to walk down a long hallway, at the end of which hung a floor-to-ceiling mirror, and each time I saw my reflection, I was shocked all over again.

The face looking back at me, dark red and cratered, felt so alien to me. Having no hair changes your appearance enormously but losing your face – the only one you've ever known – feels like a total loss of self. I just couldn't get used to how I looked now.

Metamorphosis

My first few weeks at home flew by and soon I was able to replace the splints and bandages on my hands with thin cotton gloves. The more the scabs fell away from the regenerated skin on my face, the more amazed I was at my own transformation. I often laughed when someone asked me how I was doing, declaring: 'I'm like a caterpillar in a chrysalis slowly turning into a butterfly.' That was exactly how I felt.

I'd realized that my main task now, as instructed by my teacher, was to familiarize myself with unconditional love and to live it. I also knew that the purpose of my life was to find peace through this love with the help of various experiences. I wasn't to continue adapting to the world; instead, I had to enrich it. Everything I needed to achieve this was already there, but so was everything that was holding me back.

> *Just as a caterpillar is destined*
> *to become a butterfly, love is*
> *also waiting to emerge.*

The caterpillar and the butterfly, however different they may seem, are one and the same. The caterpillar spends all day eating, unaware that a time of change is coming for it. The world it experiences in its tiny body is so limited, and it believes this is its reality. It believes that its life's purpose is to eat and grow. It feels the force of gravity and trusts its little legs to move it forward and its strong jaws to break down its food. It doesn't feel capable of more.

The caterpillar can shed its skin several times, which enables it to grow, but eventually it reaches a stage where the last layer simply cannot be released, forcing it into a transformative phase that will result in its death. Knowing that its life is coming to an end, the caterpillar looks for a quiet place to surrender to death. Its rigid skin thickens until it forms a hard cocoon, allowing the process to take place. To transform into a butterfly, the caterpillar's body must break down almost completely into its constituent parts. It soon ceases to exist, but a completely new, miraculous being develops all by itself from some of its remaining cell structures: a beautiful butterfly.

We, too, can go through a very similar metamorphosis. However, we make it much harder for ourselves than the caterpillar does because we resist it. We believe our own thoughts – those that find creative ways to tell us how powerless, small, and worthless we are. We take the nonsense we think in our mind as truth and don't realize that all the chatter and noise we hear there has absolutely nothing to do with reality.

In truth, there's nothing wrong with us at all! We're not small and powerless; we're an incredibly vast, creative, and fully connected vibrational field of the purest consciousness. We're already everything we're looking for; we just fail to recognize it in the moment because we've forgotten, just like the caterpillar, which has no idea that a second, completely different life is waiting for it.

Out in the Open

The butterfly in me showed itself through my body, which had healed miraculously, and even more clearly through the way I treated myself. Before my metamorphosis, I'd almost exclusively paid attention to other people's needs and had always put my own at the bottom of the list. Now, things were different. I was so full of energy and enthusiasm for life that I wanted to figure out what I really enjoyed doing and what felt good to me.

It all began when it occurred to me that I didn't really like many of the foods I used to eat. Around four weeks after I woke up from the coma, I decided to go to the supermarket with a friend to buy some different kinds of produce. The hair on my shaved head had barely begun to grow back, so I'd opted for a light-colored cap, and my still very sensitive hands were enclosed in thin cotton gloves. I could neither cover my face nor apply make-up to it, as it was still covered in scabs.

As we made our way around the aisles, I saw the horrified expressions on the faces of the other customers as they spotted me. Some of them gave me a sideways glance or a furtive second look, but others were less subtle, staring at me openly with mouths open.

Daring to be seen in public without a mask – in the truest sense of the word – took an incredible amount of courage. For a woman like me, who usually never left the house without make-up and was always meticulous about maintaining her appearance, it was a real challenge. But I didn't want to hide anymore.

Some of the supermarket staff who knew me approached me cautiously and expressed their sympathy. Word had got out, and a long newspaper article about my accident had done the rest. I could see how shocked they were about my predicament and how happy they were to see me again.

I could understand all these reactions. My reflection still horrified me, so how did I expect other people to feel? I did notice very quickly, however, that I felt naked and as if I was being served on a platter for everyone to dig into. But at the same time, I had a sense of calm and self-confidence that I'd never known before. After that day at the supermarket, I stopped hiding away and learned to accept myself from the outside, just as I was. It was such a liberating feeling.

Inner Changes

I faced a similar challenge, albeit not quite as great, when it came to getting dressed. Whenever I opened my wardrobe, I saw clothes that simply didn't feel like me, as if they belonged to someone who no longer existed. For example, my beloved teddy jacket, which I used to slip on as soon as I got home because it gave me a sense of security, now felt restrictive. I found its pattern irritating and I sensed in it the sadness that had accompanied me almost daily in my old life.

My inner transformation became particularly clear in these very personal areas of my life. I developed a new sensitivity to vibration, color, form, and structure, and I was struck by how attentive and kind I was to myself now. I used to wear colors that other people had recommended I wear, and I'd chosen to dress in a way that suited my job or was practical. Now, so much had changed inside me that I couldn't help but adapt my clothes to suit this change. I set about reorganizing the contents of my wardrobe and started asking myself what I'd like to wear and what I felt comfortable in.

The Magic of Letting Go

When I look back on those first few weeks and months after waking up from the coma, I can see it was a miraculous time. I remember feeling as if I'd been reborn into my old body, and I experienced the world in a completely new way. I no longer felt isolated and empty; instead, I felt fulfilled and happy.

The most amazing thing was that I hadn't consciously *done* anything to bring about this transformation. I hadn't really changed anything. Change had come naturally when I'd stopped fighting the fire and I'd stopped fighting against myself. By surrendering, I'd not only consciously welcomed death and its consequences, but I'd also relinquished control for the first time in my life. Now, my constant inner struggle had ceased because I'd made peace with myself and treated myself with love and kindness.

When I realized that everything I'd done in my life had taken me further away from myself, I let go. I made peace with all the prejudices and judgments I had about myself and the world around me. That was the only thing I'd *really* contributed to this transformation: I'd stopped trying to control my life and I'd stopped fighting, like the caterpillar surrendering to its metamorphosis. And since then, I've felt like a child discovering a completely new world for myself.

Every time I think about all the miracles that have occurred in my life since the evening of September 28, 2009, I sense the presence of my teacher. I feel his golden-yellow vibration almost to the same degree as I did during my near-death experience. It's filled me deeply, merging us until he and I cease to exist separately.

Old Me, New Me

My transformation went far beyond healing my skin, and it was so broad and sweeping that I almost felt afraid. However, I'd learned to embrace unconditionally whatever life threw at me, and that was just one of the many gifts I had to internalize. There was now an old me and a new me, and they were so utterly different that, even today, I have difficulty finding words to describe them.

How would *you* describe a state that's experienced purely through consciousness and has next to nothing to do with feelings or thoughts? A state in which you exist both in the spiritual realm and here on planet Earth in a body, living among other people? I couldn't make sense of this myself, let alone explain it to anyone, and it took me years to find the words to describe my new world.

Initially, though, it was simply a matter of learning to cope with everything that had changed, and that took time. In my old world a small and very limited version of me had lived and functioned, and she'd almost always seen herself as a victim of circumstances. Because I didn't know back then that I'd planned this life for myself before I was born and that I had the power to change everything, I felt as small and helpless as the caterpillar whose only purpose in life is to eat and grow.

However, after my near-death experience, I became a butterfly and discovered that I had wings that made it possible for me to experience the same world in a whole new way. I felt the creativity and lightness that I needed to express and was simply allowed to learn how best to make use of my wings.

Listening to My True Self

In the early days, I often tried to resume my life in the way I was familiar with, but it was a hopeless endeavor. As soon as I did something that didn't feel good or right for me, my body reacted with discomfort or even became ill. If I stayed too long in a situation where I didn't feel comfortable, my body had a way of forcing me out of it very quickly. Its favorite stop signal was to create pressure in my head or nausea. As soon as I began to ruminate and look for a way to simply function rather than truly live, the headaches started, and if necessary, my body would increase their intensity into migraines.

Although I didn't yet know why my body sometimes reacted so violently, I learned not to question it for long. I knew that it was trying to express its ethereal qualities through me in its own way, and that its reactions were a sign that I was moving away from my True Self, the spiritual part of me. My body was merely the translator, whose job it was to transform the vibration of my soul into something tangible in the material world.

During this time, I often thought back to my earlier rejection of my body. My horror when I was forced back into it during my tracheotomy surgery resurfaced, as did the many visits to its bedside with my teacher. He'd continually tried to make me aware of how wonderful my 'sacred vessel' really is. But as I've explained, I could only understand this when I recognized its connection to the Source. I was only able to accept my body when I became aware of the infinite number of dancing gold sparks in each one of my cells and felt their aliveness. It was only when I consciously engaged with all the qualities that my body possesses that I was able to recognize it as the most wonderful field of consciousness.

My own creation had become matter and it carried within it everything I needed to live a truly conscious and fulfilled life. Like the caterpillar, without which there can never be a butterfly, I can't experience fulfilment without my body. But the body is of no use to us if we don't speak its language or we ignore its loud cries, as I'd done in the past.

My teacher's words had become deeply ingrained in me, so it wasn't too difficult for me to let him guide me. 'Go back,' he'd said to me as a farewell. 'Live a full life and learn what that means for you. You'll find your way. Always carry the memory with you of the love that's at stake. Don't forget that!'

My True Self also had its very own way of communicating with me, but it was far more considerate than my body could ever be. Its method was much quieter, softer, and more loving. It put me into a state of excitement, joy, and lightness, and it gave me inspiration and ideas. It didn't trigger any of my old familiar feelings but rather an all-inclusive sense of awareness, a state of fulfilment that seemed to hold everything that existed around me and into which I could easily expand myself.

It felt exactly as it had during my near-death experience. This state of excitement wasn't comparable to any 'normal' feeling; in this state, everything felt miraculous – the air I breathed, a wooden table I touched, birds chirping, rain clouds, the diversity of nature, and pure existence itself. I suddenly saw the magic in everything, no matter what it was. And whenever I experienced this all-encompassing state, I knew that it was my True Self showing me the way.

Three Building Blocks

My time in the spiritual realm was all about learning the language of my body and my soul, and distinguishing it from my own personal thoughts and feelings. Over time, we've become an experienced team: My body shows me in no uncertain terms when I'm going in a direction that doesn't suit me, and my True Self is like a breeze that continuously flows through me, guiding me. And then there's me. I usually feel like a silent observer who receives signals from both inside and outside, and is called upon to act accordingly.

I'm like the captain of a ship, standing at the helm and guiding it in the right direction. Below me is the sea – which can be gentle or stormy, depending on its mood – and around me, the wind, which gives me direction. I've learned to hoist my sails and then lower them when the sea gets too rough.

I believe that our personality is made up of these same three key building blocks: The conscious part that always has a choice; the unconscious part that expresses itself through the body; and the spiritual part, our True Self, that gives us direction. With the help of these three building blocks, I've learned to recognize and experience the magic of my new life in each and every moment.

CHAPTER 16

A Radical Transformation

Shortly before Christmas 2009, my physical condition had improved so much that I found it difficult to relax or sit still. Almost three months had passed since the accident and even though I still had to be very careful with my hands, I really needed to do something again. I was constantly overcome by an uncontrollable urge to tidy up. I wanted to throw things away, to rearrange and reorganize, because I felt nothing fitted me anymore.

My material possessions seemed drab, old, and restrictive. The contents of every drawer and shelf ended up on the floor and I took a ruthless approach to ridding myself of anything that no longer meant anything to me. It struck me that there wasn't much that I was really attached to unless it was linked to a happy memory. Again and again, I asked myself whether I really needed an item or object, whether I liked having it around, or whether it was good for me. It's truly amazing how many meaningless items you retain in a bid to fill an inner void.

All the gifts I'd brought back with me from my trip to the spiritual world couldn't be tidied away, and yet the memories of every single moment I'd spent there were the most precious thing I possessed. So, one garbage bag after another quickly made its way out the front of the house, and with each one I felt increasingly free.

Withdrawing

I'd noticed for some time that I required a lot of space and time for myself. I was finding it increasingly difficult to participate in idle chit-chat anyway, so I skillfully avoided it. I could barely bring myself to listen and talk to my husband when he told me the latest news or wanted to hear my opinion on some political issue or other. And the stories my friends told me felt as trivial as the programs on TV.

Everything around me seemed so devoid of content, so empty and superficial, and I was becoming less and less interested in engaging with it at all. It took an incredible amount of energy to follow a conversation about something that didn't interest me, because it seemed it was always about some drama or issue that was no longer relevant to me.

There were no more dramas for me – neither in my head nor in my feelings. Instead, I experienced everything around me as a part of the same miracle: the snow that gently transforms any landscape into a winter wonderland; the smell of freshly baked potatoes; the feel of wood and certain fabrics.... Instead of watching TV or reading, I found it much more fulfilling to look out the window for hours or go for a walk. Spending time in nature made me feel fully connected to my new world. I was simply overjoyed to be alive again.

As I explained earlier, during my near-death experience, I'd felt unconditional love everywhere, and I was completely woven into it. There were no limits in the spiritual realm; I was free to explore my own infinity. Worlds opened as and when I wanted them to. Back in my body and in our material world, I was suddenly bound by its laws once more, and increasingly I felt out of place.

In moments like these, I'd often retreat to a quiet place and let myself fall back into the loving energy of my teacher without being distracted. I sought his advice and explanations for my feelings because I realized that I was slowly but surely withdrawing from almost everything that had once been so important to me. Nothing had the same meaning as before my near-death experience, and that was deeply unsettling.

Whenever I took the time to consciously connect with my teacher and fully immerse myself, the space around me faded away. My body would begin to tingle inside, as if I had champagne bubbles inside me – such an incredible feeling! Everything became so light, limitless, and free, unlike the real world around me. He'd take me in his arms, and gently help me to adjust to his high vibration, which I knew so well. It felt as if, with his help, I could slip beyond my material world and its limits, and easily leave my body.

A Book with Empty Pages

On one occasion, I asked him, 'Why is everything so different in my life all of a sudden? Everything in me just marvels at the miracle of life, and I feel unbelievably happy about it all! Not a loud, exuberant happiness, but a quiet peace that makes me deeply contented.

'However, because of all that's happening to me, I also feel so alone. Everything that meant anything to me in my old life has lost its meaning. Everything that's going on in the world, all the issues that other people are dealing with, seem so insignificant to me. I feel like a book with all these empty pages that need to be filled and I don't know how to fill them or what to fill them with,' I concluded my rant.

My teacher listened to me attentively because he knew how difficult these changes were for me to comprehend. 'What a beautiful and very fitting image, Anke!' he replied. 'If you feel like a book with empty pages now, do you remember how you felt before we met?'

'Barely. I know that version of me existed, and I know how she felt, but I can't empathize with those feelings anymore; I don't have access to them. It's a bit like amnesia but for my feelings,' I explained. 'Before, almost everything in my life was tedious and difficult, and all I could see were problems. I felt pressure from everything, but I put the most pressure on myself because I kept thinking I had to change, to adapt myself to the world.

'I didn't like myself and therefore I didn't like my life, and that's precisely what's so unbelievably different now. I see everything through completely different eyes; it's as if I've been sleepwalking all my life, as if I've been living among other sleepwalkers and I've suddenly woken up.'

'You went beyond the limits of your lower self when you realized who you really are,' my teacher reminded me. 'During those nine days, you moved beyond everything you'd previously accepted as your reality, and that's precisely why you're now experiencing yourself and your world in a totally different, new way. With your consciousness, you experienced realms beyond your former perspective, and now it's no longer possible for you to return to your old, limited world. Do you remember what I told you about that?'

'Yes, of course!' I replied. You said, "When the invisible becomes visible, you can never fall back into ignorance."'

'That's right. You alone can choose the angle from which you view your life and decide what you want to discover. I want to show you what I mean by that. It's only now that you're in your body again that you can really grasp the true meaning of my words. You'll also understand why you see yourself and the world through different eyes.'

Expanding Our Cocoon

Once more, I found myself in the elevated vantage point I'd come to know so well since meeting my teacher. Pictures and experiences, and insights about those experiences, appeared in my consciousness, as if he was trying to filter out specific aspects from the many things that we'd already looked at together. As I had before, I saw the thick, impenetrable cocoon that had separated me from the higher levels of my soul. But this time my teacher wanted to show me how it functions using a different image.

I saw a snow globe – a beautiful sphere containing a tiny, magical, sealed-off world of its own in which there was day and night, light and shadow, thoughts and feelings, space and time. Everything that I'd believed was my reality prior to September 28, 2009 existed within this snow globe. My teacher asked me to enter it, and as soon as I did, my perception changed, and I began to re-identify with the world within it. The snow globe contained everything I thought of myself – all my experiences, adventures, and thoughts. All my old feelings suddenly came flooding back and I began to see the world in a very similar way to how I had before the accident.

Once more, I felt like a sole entity – a clearly defined individual with a body. All the familiar doubts hit me at once, as well as joy and fear. A sense of time existed here, a past and a future into which the limitlessness in which I'd been immersed – thanks to my teacher – faded away.

A Small, Distorted World

I then noticed that the inside of the snow globe was mirrored. While it was possible to get an unobstructed view into the globe from the outside, you couldn't look out from the inside. From within this limited, self-reflecting world, it was impossible for me to see that something much greater, something infinitely more creative, was outside of me.

The longer I spent there, the more isolated and separated I became from my teacher; whenever I looked for him, all I saw was my own reflection. I felt disconnected from *connectedness*, unconditional existence, and higher purpose. And that was when I fully comprehended how the cocoon works: Everything we refer to as the ego takes place within it and its primary task is to 'filter' our consciousness so that we can experience ourselves purely through our bodies, our feelings, and our thoughts.

This process is like extreme amnesia. The cocoon continuously splits our consciousness from the higher, spiritual realm, creating the illusion of separation. As I explained earlier, this is the only possible way for us to experience human feelings and to develop a thinking mind (more on this in the next chapter).

> *The more we focus our consciousness on*
> *the body and our lower self, the more*
> *we forget our home, the Source.*

We forget where we've come from, where we're returning to, and that all of this is an illusion into which we've consciously placed ourselves. The mirrored inside of the cocoon draws all our attention inward. It makes us feel separate and think we're alone, while also giving us a sense of security and direction in this brand-new world.

A Bigger, Less Restricted View

For the most part, we're all inside our own cocoon, our consciousness trapped within its confines, and this is what we consider to be our reality. But as life progresses, we begin to question this reality. My guess is that you want to look behind the mirror of your cocoon, too, otherwise you wouldn't be reading this book. Maybe you've prayed to God, sought contact with the angels, or pursued a higher wisdom that you knew resided within you. No matter what path you've pursued with your consciousness up to now, everything took place within your cocoon.

The more aware you become of your True Self, and the more experiences of connectedness you encounter on your path, the more your cocoon – your old, limited world – will expand. Obstacles that seemed insurmountable suddenly cease to exist. Doubts and fears that used to prevent you from taking another step toward your True Self vanish into thin air.

Each time you see through an illusion, be it a fear or an old belief, your cocoon expands, creating more space inside it, and with that its mirror gradually fades. The more we know our True Self and let ourselves be guided by it, the more our cocoon expands – and with it our consciousness. The more we perceive the world through the eyes of our soul, the more miracles we witness.

Those who, as I did, focus their attention on the outside find that the inner workings of their cocoon are mostly very limiting. This probably makes it thicker, tighter, and darker, just like mine, and makes the longing to break free from it grow ever greater.

The mirror inside the cocoon prevents almost all of us from recognizing, feeling, and becoming one with our True Self. We don't see that everything we long for is within our reach. We look at the world through the eyes of our lower self and that's why we feel powerless. We have no idea that it's about understanding the mirror for what it is, so we're then able to see through it and into the realm beyond it.

This is exactly what happened to me during my near-death experience. The mirror, which had only ever showed me my own deep-rooted thoughts and feelings, suddenly dissolved. I was not only freed from the confines of my body, but also from my cocoon, allowing me to immerse myself in all the things that exist outside of it. For this reason alone, I was able to expand infinitely – with the help of my teacher, of course – and to recognize my True Self so comprehensively.

Finding My Way

The radical transformation I'd experienced thanks to my near-death experience was anything but easy – in fact, it felt like jumping into ice-cold water. The two worlds I inhabited couldn't have been more different. However, I'd never been so happy and fulfilled, and I felt safe in the knowledge that I was connected to everything.

The mirror inside my snow globe had disappeared because I'd broken through it. Everything that it had hidden from my consciousness suddenly became visible – and it stayed that way. There were no limits for me after that because I'd retained the ability to expand my consciousness at will into all the areas I'd experienced – and that was truly mind-blowing.

I knew what the people around me were thinking, what they were feeling, and where and why they had illness in their bodies. When I looked at a tree, or decided what to wear or eat, I saw the energetic vibration of matter. Whatever I looked at, it transformed right before my eyes as soon as I shifted my gaze. In the same way, I was also able to focus on myself and my body, however I wanted to. This experience threw overboard everything I'd previously considered to be 'true' or 'real.'

If I'd been a hermit, I'd have spent the next few years just marveling at the world around me, but I had a family and friends, a job, and what you'd call a work routine – and that was the biggest challenge for me. I couldn't muster the courage to talk to anyone about what was happening to me. Of course, I made a few cautious attempts to tell my family and friends about my changed perception, but I was quickly silenced when I saw their puzzled looks. I felt so scared and confused by it all.

Seeing Through the Illusion

When the invisible becomes visible or, more precisely, tangible, everything that was right before no longer fits. As soon as you've seen through a magician's tricks, no matter how brilliant they are, their performance no longer has any effect on you. In my life, I'd been surrounded by people who, like me before the accident, saw the material world as the only 'real' reality; people who didn't want to know about the illusions that were being performed so cleverly and who continued to take pleasure in the magic show of 'reality.'

I think that describes my entire personal predicament quite well. For me, this solid, material world still existed. Take touching a table as an example – I could feel it, but in addition to that, I also saw its elementary particles dancing and sensed that I could reach through them at any time. And death triggered a compassionate joy in me rather than fear. I saw the challenges that we encounter in life as a wonderful opportunity to expand our cocoon, and to me, fear was just one of the cocoon's magic tricks.

No matter what tragedies occurred in the world or in my personal surroundings, I was no longer able to interpret them. When you see everything from a state of heightened consciousness, all you can see is love; you recognize the creative process of experience in everything that happens. In this way of looking at things, nothing is 'good' or 'bad,' 'fortunate' or 'unfortunate.' I learned to recognize the higher purpose in everything that happened, no matter how tragic it seemed, and the possibilities that came with it.

Since my sense of time had also changed drastically, I struggled to project my thoughts into the future or to rummage around in the past. I was simply in the here and now, seizing the moment and everything within it in a state of infinite gratitude. However, since the people around me knew nothing of any of this, they thought I was a little strange. They noticed the change in me, of course, but because I didn't talk about it, they blamed it on my 'traumatic experience.'

All of this was the reason why, as I'd told my teacher, I felt like a book with empty pages. The limitations that had seemed so real to me in my old life or to my lower, unconscious self, had dissolved. The challenge now was to live with an unlimited consciousness in a limited world and to find my way in it.

I begged my teacher for help. 'What am I supposed to do now? Can you please just tell me how to deal with my family and friends, so I feel like I belong again? How can I go on like this?' Changing my diet or my clothes was easy, and clearing out my possessions also helped, but I'd reached a point where I really didn't know what to do. I wanted to redesign my life and consciously live out all the fulfilment I felt inside, but I didn't know how.

'Live out the Source within you,' was his curt response. 'Stop resisting and allow yourself to be guided. Then you'll find your way.'

This answer wasn't quite as satisfying as I'd hoped because I couldn't really figure out what it meant. But that was all I was going to get from him, and so I trusted that the right path would show up of its own accord.

CHAPTER 17

Living Out Fulfilment

As the months turned into a year, I found myself increasingly able to settle into the old – and the new – world. My face and ears had miraculously healed all by themselves, and when my hair had fully regrown, I was finally able to recognize myself in the mirror.

Today, most people are shocked when they hear how severe my injuries were because you can't tell what I've been through just by looking at me. A small scar above my upper lip and a slight difference in color on my hands are the only sign of the third-degree burns I suffered. My body hadn't needed plastic surgery, nor had it required a face mask made of compression material or anything else for my skin to renew itself.

My eyes are the only part of my body that's altered completely – they used to be dull and lifeless, but now they shine. They sparkle with love and life as soon as I start talking about all the miracles that we hold within us. They're like a gateway into the bright light of the worlds I speak of so passionately, or at least that's how it feels to me sometimes.

Much of my life changed over time – and of its own accord – as I learned to listen to my body and follow the feeling of lightness within me. As soon as I stopped trying to control something, a solution or sometimes even a change of direction appeared as if by magic. In my old life, making big, important decisions would have triggered unbelievable anxiety and fear in me because it threatened my enormous need for security. I would never have dared to engage with life without having full control; I would never have faced up to its challenges, because I was terrified of the unknown.

But I knew that I'd only returned to this body to express the creative being that I truly am. I'd realized that my True Self knows no resistance, fear, or confinement, as these parts of me are in a permanent state of unconditionality. I wanted to learn to live out this unconditionality in my new life. I never again wanted to be unloving to myself; I never again wanted to spend my time doing things that didn't feel good, things I didn't even want to do; and I didn't want to live in a way that went against my true nature. However, I didn't yet know how best to implement this self-knowledge.

Expressing My True Self

As I touched on earlier, for far too long I'd looked at the outside world as the standard and tried to adapt myself to it. I'd only ever focused on the world around me, which, for the most part, I'd found difficult and intimidating. I'd compared myself to people I admired, tried to live up to society's expectations, and allowed others to show me what the limits were.

I'd looked at the world through the eyes of my lower, unconscious self, and living in this way takes an enormous amount of energy because we're constantly trying to adapt to external circumstances. We judge everything we do or don't do and become our own worst critic. If we always react to the countless influences in the world around us instead of being at peace with ourselves, we soon start to feel overwhelmed.

However, as soon as you recognize your True Self within you, you begin to look at your life from a completely new perspective. You automatically withdraw your attention from the outside world and begin to focus it on yourself. You stop asking yourself what others want, and instead start asking yourself what feels good and what feels easy.

As soon as you begin to value yourself,
all the miracles you hold within you
start to feel available to you.

As soon as you realize that your life is all about making decisions for yourself and that you live your life for you and you alone, everything changes. That's exactly what I did. Without exception, I questioned everything that had taken up so much space in my life and finally started paying attention to my needs.

Did I *really* want that this or that thing? Did it feel light, or did it make my body feel heavy and under pressure? What made me excited and what took effort? Everything was put to the test: my marriage, my friendships, and my behavior in various situations; I thoroughly questioned anything that made me feel uncomfortable.

There were two questions in particular that I asked myself: *Why am I behaving like this? Why am I allowing myself to feel this way?* The answers that arose automatically in me clearly reflected my old struggle for survival. In most cases, they were: *because I want to be loved; because I want to belong;* and *because I'm afraid of being powerless.*

During my near-death experience, however, I'd realized that none of these thoughts and feelings corresponded to the truth. They were all based on past experiences and had nothing to do with my True Self. Being outside my body had shown me that I'm always and unconditionally connected to everything, and that any sense of separation, lack, or powerlessness I'd felt had been created by my own limited self-perception.

The Lightness Within

As I've said, in the past, I'd never have dared to take any kind of drastic action because I trusted myself far too little. I was afraid of making important decisions because I thought I'd make a mistake. I worried that I'd take a wrong turn, lose something valuable, or feel powerless in the face of uncertain situations. Almost everything in my life was shaped by these fears and insecurities, and they prevented me from expressing my True Self.

However, it got easier when I understood that life is all about recognizing and following the creative being within. During my near-death experience, I'd seen that heaviness, pressure, fear, and resistance exist only in our human consciousness and serve as signals to let us know when we're living life in a way that doesn't correspond to our True Self.

As soon as we judge ourselves,
listen to our fears, or resist something,
we know that we've lost our connection
to the Source within us.

In these situations, our mind's old, habitual patterns or distraction strategies have triumphed, and we've forgotten that we always have the choice to continue to follow them or not. Once I'd recognized that I have the chance to completely reshape my life at any given moment, and that it's up to me and me alone how I experience myself and the world around me, I was able to take countermeasures.

Making Big Decisions

After a few teething problems, I came to really enjoy exposing my resistance and overwriting it with new decisions. I knew I couldn't go wrong if I listened to the lightness within me, and that gave me courage. In the spiritual realm I'd learned that I could change everything I'd created unconsciously in the past using just my attention, and now it was simply a question of implementing it.

As soon as I found anything difficult or felt pressure or fear, I knew I was about to fall back into an old habit. In almost every one of these situations, it was enough to ask myself just one question: *Do I really want to feel like this?* Since the answer was usually an immediate no, I had only to ask: *How do I want to feel instead?* And then act on the result. The magical thing was that everything else seemed to happen almost automatically and all I needed to do was observe the changes.

I noticed this with my marriage, especially. My husband and I had been married for 16 years, but we'd grown apart and all that really connected us was our son, Manuel, and dealing with day-to-day life. Our relationship was more a loving partnership of convenience than a romantic one, and now, this just wasn't enough for me. When I realized this, he and I talked about it, and it became clear to both of us that we'd fulfilled our mutual roles in life. We separated and, for me, this was a natural next step on the path to becoming myself.

Challenging the Thinker

During my recovery, something else happened to me and it was, unfortunately, less conscious, and very subtle. Since everything in my old life had lost its value, I was looking for a new direction and I yearned for focus. I wanted a different profession, one that would fulfil me and give meaning to my new life.

My teacher wasn't much help; he didn't respond when I asked him what I should do next. Despite not having an answer, I was determined to make a new life for myself that was full of value, so I read countless books, attended seminars, and listened to lectures. Through other people's experiences I hoped to be shown a path that I could take myself. However, this approach backfired.

When we think about what we really want in life, our head starts spinning. The thinker in us becomes active and tries to present us with a suitable answer, but it soon reaches its limit. It's so focused on the past that it fails to access all the limitless qualities that are present in our True Self. The thinker has carefully organized all our experiences into drawers, weighed up the pros and cons, and evaluated them to solve our problems.

Because in the past I'd never really concerned myself with my desires or the possibilities open to me, the thinker couldn't present me with a suitable solution now, either. It had next to no drawers to access, and this was precisely where my biggest challenge lay. The more I looked outside myself for a solution, the more often I got a headache; my heart raced too, and I felt sick to my stomach. This search dragged on for months and became increasingly difficult. The more books and other content I consumed, the more possibilities my mind presented to me, but somehow none of them felt right.

Your Records Are Being Deleted

Eventually, change was heralded by an intense dream in which I saw myself alone in a dark valley with nothing for miles around except a huge, fierce bonfire. The closer I got to the fire, the more I could see why it blazed so powerfully – countless books were burning on it, and as if by magic, new ones kept appearing.

I wondered what kind of books they were, and no sooner had I thought this did one fly straight at my feet. It was the book I was currently reading. Another looked like a diary from my childhood, which fell to pieces before my eyes. A huge library with endless shelves and countless books then appeared – old books, new books, big books and small books, and each one was important and personal to me.

I watched in horror as they tumbled one by one from the shelves into the fire, where they burst into flames. Any attempt to save them was doomed to failure, for the fire was much stronger than I was. 'What on earth is this? What's going on?' I shouted at the flames in my dream. 'Your records are being permanently deleted,' was the answer I received.

I woke up from this dream feeling exhausted and it took me some time to calm down. What I'd seen in it triggered fear in me – fear of forgetting myself when the books ceased to exist; fear of not knowing what to do without my 'records'; even a fear that I myself would cease to exist when I no longer had access to the books. I sat on the terrace in my bathrobe with a cup of coffee and let the dream sink in. What did 'your records are being deleted' mean? I'd learned that it was almost always enough to simply ask myself a question and then calmly wait for the answer to come. Perhaps all these books, my 'records,' were my experiences, my saved experiences? My thoughts, even?

The explanation that emerged surprised me almost as much as the dream itself because it felt so real. Suddenly, everything I'd experienced over the last few months made sense, both my physical reactions and my desperate search for direction. The bottom line was that I was well on the way to losing my connection with the Source within me and becoming a sleepwalker again.

I hadn't been listening to my body or my soul and instead I'd looked to my teacher or the authors of all those books to give me a to-do list. I'd given up my power and wanted to follow other people on their path instead of discovering my own. I'd started to think, and therefore I'd lost the magic of the moment. 'Live out the Source within you. Stop resisting and let yourself be guided,' my teacher had advised me, but I'd done the exact opposite. The thinker in me had desperately tried to find a solution, but that was impossible if I wanted to live out the Source within me.

I understood then why I so often suffered from headaches. My body wanted me to stop thinking and ruminating as I tried to plan out my future, and to trust in my sense of ease and let joy guide me. Instead of relying on myself and my inner wisdom, I'd tried to follow a leader – any leader – like a sheep. The books in my dream represented all the memories, experiences, beliefs, and answers that I'd collected in my life so far. I quickly discovered the 'solution' to my dilemma because it was obvious.

Giving Up Control

It was only a few days after this dream that I noticed I was struggling to remember things. It felt as if my memory had sprung a leak; I couldn't remember why I'd gone to the supermarket, and I kept getting lost when I was trying to go places. The thinker in me seemed to have gone on permanent leave. I Googled the symptoms of amnesia; I didn't know what exactly happened to me on the night of the fire, but since then my mind seemed to have taken on a whole new role. I could barely remember anything to do with facts, figures, or times, because it just didn't seem important anymore.

I also had trouble recalling past events, no matter how dramatic or impactful they may have been. Instead, my mind seemed to be constantly set to 'receive' in a completely different way. It translated the vibrations I perceived into more tangible information and protected me from mental overstimulation. I could use it when I was looking for the solution to a problem, but most of the time it worked silently in the background. It felt wonderfully light.

The lesson of the dream had a significant impact on my life. I put away all my books, stopped listening to lectures, and stopped worrying about my future. In the process, I came to the most important realization of all: As soon as I *let go* of everything – all the things I think I must do to find myself – all that I am already will come to me by itself.

Now, I also understood my teacher's silence on the subject. He'd given me the opportunity to discover for myself that I didn't want to control my life anymore. I realized that I couldn't possibly know what miracles life had in store for me, so I gave up trying to figure it out. I gave up trying to plan things in advance; I gave up needing to know and to have control, and I surrendered to the present moment.

Reconciling Two Realities

The way I see it, it's the thinker in us – or our limiting beliefs about ourselves – that keeps us from connecting with our True Self. I once thought it was impossible for me to live a happy and fulfilled life because I just didn't know how. I looked up to and greatly admired people who had already achieved the goal of happiness and fulfilment, but it had always felt unattainable for myself.

After the nine surreal days I spent in a coma, receiving all the knowledge and answers I'd been seeking all my life, I still had a huge challenge ahead of me: I had to figure out how I could implement everything that I'd learned in the spiritual realm in our limited material world. As I mentioned earlier, when I found myself back in my body, it was quite difficult, especially at the beginning, because two realities coexisted for me, and they were both so very different.

One was within my mind, and the other reached far beyond the confines of my mind. The mind is constantly trying to understand – it wants to make connections and to make us act. If we take our cues from it, we find ourselves constantly asking what we can do, what we should change, and how best to act. Then we try to put in to practice what it's helped us to recognize.

Conversely, in the spiritual realm we find ourselves in an all-encompassing state of *being* in which we view everything like a wise and kind mother looking upon her child with unconditional love and affection. She recognizes the child's full potential and lovingly lets them have their own experiences without trying to influence them. A caring observer, she gently nudges her child in the right direction when she notices they're getting lost.

Our True Self speaks to us through impulses,
inspirations, and ideas that always feel
light, uplifting, enriching, and positive.

That was the first key I needed at the time to reconcile these two worlds. We're all familiar with the lightness and positivity I've described: It shows itself very clearly to us during various phases of our lives. For example, when we fall in love, the world around us feels so light and breezy. A rainy day is suddenly the most glorious day we've ever had, simply because we're bursting with happiness and see love all around us. In this state, anything seems possible, and our inner joy has no limits.

However, this blissful state of happiness usually only lasts until the thinker in us begins to interfere, cautiously asking whether the other person really loves us as much as we love them. From that moment on, our head starts spinning and we're faced with our fears. If we're unlucky, our good mood will suddenly dissipate.

I bet there have been moments in your life when you've had a wonderful idea or made a significant decision for yourself, and then the detail just figures itself out. As if by magic, you meet the right people, find the perfect job, or suddenly come into money when you really need it. As if a higher power were pulling invisible strings, everything falls into place, and in awe, you just stand and watch it all unfold. This is the exact guidance we receive from our True Self, and it usually comes when we've either stopped thinking or when we haven't even started.

Spreading the Word

For a long time after my near-death experience, I remained in that incredibly blissful and all-encompassing state from which I'd originated. I had next to no real sense of the space around me, and time didn't matter either. Everything felt so light, and the two worlds seemed to have completely merged into one.

I then learned to follow the feeling of lightness by cutting out everything from my life that didn't feel good. I stopped engaging in conversations that left me devoid of energy, and I detached myself from people whose presence didn't make me feel right. In doing so I learned to respect my own needs; I viewed myself lovingly and kindly, and made sure I felt comfortable.

My thinker rarely interfered in this process because I rarely gave it a chance to do so. That only changed when I started to think about how I could create a new life for myself and give it real meaning. Whenever I asked myself what I'd most like to do, there was only one answer: I want to show people what I've been through. I want to show them what they're made of. I want to bring them closer to these miracles and tell them that although we're all living in an incomprehensible illusion, there's a way to break through it!

I wanted to start sharing all this right away, but I didn't know how. Since I struggled to put these miracles into words and my teacher was hardly much help, I started to think. I read books by other people who had experienced similar things and tried to find a solution to my problem with reason. I can't help but smile as I write this, because I know now that my only 'problem' was that I simply didn't know how to bring this inner enthusiasm to the outside world.

From today's perspective, that phase of my life was extremely educational, and I feel eternally grateful that my teacher didn't just hand me the answer on a silver platter. This was the only way I could experience how easy it is to lose the connection to the Source just by thinking. If I'd known back then that I didn't need to rack my brain trying to figure out what my path was, I could have made life so much easier for myself. But then I'd have also deprived myself of important lessons and knowledge.

PART IV

The Path to Our True Self

CHAPTER 18

The Eight Golden Keys to Life

In this book, I've made a modest attempt to tell you about the eternity that exists within you, but I'm aware that I've barely scratched the surface. I also know, however, that a very large part of you will have absorbed every vibration in these pages. I've captured the essence of what I wanted to tell you through my own story. Did you feel it? Maybe you couldn't put the book down as you came on this journey with me. Maybe you've noticed that it's had some effect on you that you can sense in your own special way.

Have you realized that you and I are *connected*? Yes, that's right – if we weren't, you wouldn't be holding this book right now. It wouldn't have resonated with you; you simply wouldn't have found it appealing, or you'd have set it aside after reading a few pages. But something inside you drew you to the book, didn't it?

It was probably the part of you that's been longing to show you the path to your personal truth.

As you now know, I'm very familiar with what it's like to long for a fulfilling life. It hurts, especially when you're convinced that you'll never get there, no matter what you do. Never in my wildest dreams did I think I'd write a book that reveals the miracles that are waiting to be discovered in this life. I'd never have thought it possible for me to exist outside of my body, or to consciously recognize the Source within me.

What I want you to know is quite simple: No matter where you are in your life right now, no matter how you feel or what you think of yourself, there's a part of you that has an incredible amount of love for you – a higher power that's capable of making the miracles you long for in your reality.

You don't have to die to experience it. You don't have to survive an accident, illness, or even a near-death experience to see yourself and your life as the miracle it is. You don't need to communicate with the higher power I speak of or to look for it outside yourself because it's already within you and all around you, and it always has been.

In the time that's passed since that momentous day in September 2009, I've learned to use the eight golden keys to a fulfilling life that my teacher taught me. I brought them with me into my new life and have been using them daily ever since. I've learned to see myself as the spiritual being my teacher revealed I was. I know now that I've always carried these golden keys inside me – even before any of this happened. I'd simply forgotten, just as *you* have.

Key 1: Surrender and Accept

My whole journey began with surrender and acceptance, and they've been prominent themes in my life ever since. Surrender and acceptance are the master keys that fit any lock, and there are aspects of them in the other seven golden keys. The more we learn to surrender to life and accept it for what it is, the more miracles it will show us.

But what does it mean to surrender and accept? In my case, when I lost control of the fire that had engulfed my body, I consciously surrendered to a higher power. For the first time in my life, I'd decided to use this golden key, making this a magical, decisive moment. I gave up my desperate struggle and surrendered to death and the complete unknown; I *accepted* what was happening. If I'd acted differently in that moment, I probably wouldn't have had the experiences that followed it. Someone like me, who had always tried to control everything, likely needed to be *forced* to surrender in this way. I was relinquishing control, and I didn't care what happened to me.

In the simplest terms, surrendering means ending your inner struggle and giving up the fight. When you surrender, you stop running up against walls and trying to change things that simply cannot be altered. Surrender is the golden key we can use in any situation where we find ourselves desperately trying to change something, whether that's at work, with our family, or something else in our lives. Our inner battles drain us of energy and exhaust us; sometimes, they even make us feel hopeless because, if we're honest, we're always fighting against ourselves.

But we have the choice to change everything at any moment. We can continue to make our lives difficult by trying to overcome invisible hurdles, or we can simply go with life's flow and surrender to it. Life simply mirrors our own view; it never works against us. In the moments when I can't surrender, I end up fighting against myself. I listen to my inner voice or the fear within me and freeze inside my cocoon. But as soon as I see through the insidious game my ego/the cocoon is playing, I surrender. I stop fighting imaginary evils and ask my True Self for a solution. And trust me, the answer always comes.

Never forget that you don't have to fight.
As soon as you surrender, you're free.

Surrendering is the most difficult thing in the world if you *aim* to surrender, because your mind will find an infinite number of ways to prevent you from truly doing so. But if you just let it happen, if you *allow* yourself to surrender, then it's the easiest path of all. To surrender is to truly acknowledge and appreciate everything – yourself, your life, and its circumstances. Surrender is a process of self-awareness. Through surrendering, you learn to accept yourself and your life just as they are, in the present moment.

Key 2: Practice Gratitude

Gratitude is one of the most important golden keys for living a fulfilling life because it's a declaration of love. The gratitude I'm talking about isn't a feeling in the conventional sense, but more a state of mind that comes from an awareness of the qualities you already possess. We all have an infinite amount of gratitude within us, and it would fulfil us if we weren't so quick to dismiss it as unremarkable or not worthy of mention.

So often, we regard our achievements, successes, inner values, and wonderful character traits as 'nothing special.' I was a master at it myself. Today, however, I see in this attitude a lack of appreciation, a coldness. No matter what I'd achieved, no matter what hurdles I'd overcome, it didn't matter – and that's why it was never enough. *I* was never enough for myself. I was never worthy.

I certainly didn't act from a place of gratitude, which shows how little I valued myself. What about you? Do you appreciate yourself? Do you appreciate how you laugh or cry when something moves you? Do you appreciate that you're a good listener, that you're compassionate? Are you grateful to yourself for reconciling with certain people in your life? Can you accept compliments or gifts? Do you recognize that you're there for others when they need you? Are you able to ask for help when you need it?

Do you take care of yourself and your needs? Have you opened space within yourself that you didn't have before? Can you be proud of yourself and the path you've taken in life? Are you proud of all the challenges you've already overcome? Are you thankful for your sense of adventure and daring? Your zest for life? Are you grateful for your tolerance toward other people and your courage when it comes to setting boundaries? Do you look back on your life and see all the things you've already achieved?

It's actually quite easy to practice gratitude: When you *focus* on the abundance within you and your life, you begin to *notice* abundance everywhere. Similarly, if you focus on lack, then that's what you experience. If you make a habit of practicing gratitude, you'll learn to love yourself and your life. There's no other way. You'll start to value yourself, and your self-love will lead to a state of fulfilment. Other people will react to your positive energy and reflect it back at you: love reflects love.

You'll feel more balanced and stable, and experience an inner harmony that you weren't aware of before. You'll attract situations and opportunities from the field of infinite possibilities, which you'd never allowed yourself to access before. You'll feel an inner peace in every area of your life and gratitude for that inner peace.

Gratitude is a state of fulfilment and a
declaration of love for yourself and your
life. Gratitude is a state of being.

The state of gratitude I exist in today is amazing because I constantly feel as if I could burst with joy. I'm eternally grateful to be alive; to be able to breathe, enjoy food, hug my son, and hear the birds sing. I'm grateful for so many other things, too, like running water and the first snow of the year. *None* of this is a given. Please, never forget that *you* are not a given.

I'm eternally grateful to the fire for giving me the opportunity to leave my body and have that eye-opening experience in the spiritual realm. I feel immense gratitude toward myself for being open to it and allowing it to happen, as well as for all the challenges that came with it. I'm grateful to my teacher and my parents. I feel this gratitude in every moment, in all areas of my life. Nothing is exempt.

Key 3: Know That You Always Have a Choice

During my experience, whether I was in the spiritual realm with my teacher or in my physical body, one thing was constant: I always had, and always will have, a choice. I can choose to fight against myself or to surrender. I can choose to do things that don't feel good to me, or I can choose to not do them. I can choose to submit and feel small and powerless, or I can decide to stop. *Now*. It's entirely up to me how I perceive my life and what I pay attention to. I *always* have a choice.

And *you* always have the choice to change your life. You're not powerless or helpless; you're an incredibly rich field of consciousness with endless possibilities at your disposal. Stop making yourself small and remember your True Self!

> *Never forget that you are in*
> *control of your own life.*

When I tell you that you always have a choice, I'm addressing this unconscious part of you. The truth is, it doesn't matter whether you have fears or insecurities or already trust yourself to make changes to your life. Now, in this moment, I just want you to know that you can change things in an instant, and in whichever way you see fit – even if you don't yet know *how*.

Our consciousness uses our attention to create our reality, both in the higher spiritual realm and in our limited material world. This means that we're inevitably and permanently the creators of our own reality. We shape our own lives, and we can achieve certain things by focusing on certain areas. We manifest things all the time because that's simply our nature.

Exercising choice is nothing more than making a decision, and we make decisions all the time. However, most of them are unconscious decisions, and as soon as we've recognized this, we can take countermeasures. We can find out what we really want, what fulfils us, and what makes us feel good. But it's up to us whether we decide to follow the fear within us or not; whether we continue to play the victim because it's easier and more comfortable than the alternative or finally take responsibility for ourselves.

As soon as we realize that every 'I can't do it' and 'That's impossible' are just fears rearing their ugly heads, we can detach ourselves from them. With each conscious decision we make, we reconnect with our True Self. The next golden key will help you to make these decisions in a very simple and magical way.

Key 4: Make a Decision

This key is pure magic, and once you start using it, you'll be amazed. It'll teach you to experience lightness and joy, and to recognize life itself as a miracle. Don't believe me? Then allow me to elaborate. This key allows your True Self to remain in constant communication with you because it takes the wind out of the sails of your inner thinker.

What would it be like if you never had to worry about *how* you're going to achieve everything you want in life? What if it was enough to simply *decide* what you want and then *wait* for all the changes you want to see become reality?

What if a much wiser part of you took care of your requests? A part of you that takes every single thought you have and turns it into reality. Can you imagine that? Do you even think it's possible? If so, you're already well on your way to using the fourth golden key to attract the magic you crave into your life. You don't need to know *how* – you can just *decide* what you want and then let your True Self (or Creation/God) take care of it.

Thus far, overthinking and rumination are the reasons why the negative beliefs that your inner thinker has churned out have become your reality. Because what you think, you create. If you don't think you can do it, then you're right. What you *think* will happen is exactly what *will* happen. For example, if you're convinced that you don't deserve happiness, then you'll certainly have more than enough opportunities to confirm this belief. If you're convinced that you can't lose weight, then it's going to be difficult for you to do so.

Never forget that you're always right.
If you think your life is hard, then it will
be hard. But if you believe in miracles,
your life will be a miracle too!

This is what always happens and it's part of our intrinsic nature. Since we're beings who are made up of pure vibration, we're subject to the laws of the universe. And since we're creative consciousness, we can't help but create and manifest things. Energy flows where attention goes, and you're constantly attracting into your reality the things that you pay most attention to. Whether you do it consciously or unconsciously, it doesn't change anything.

But not needing to know *how* is a magical key that can influence the thinker in you; it bypasses the filter that's separated you from your own higher power and allows your True Self to support you on a path that will bring growth into your life. By no longer relying on the thinker in you to fulfil a decision, your True Self can let things that correspond to your wishes – and perhaps even things far beyond them – become reality.

If you choose an easy path, you'll experience an easy path. If you choose a path that enables you to understand more complex connections, that's what you'll get. It really doesn't matter what you choose because not only do you always have a choice, you also always get what you're convinced you're going to get.

Key 5: Understand Your True Purpose

Perhaps, like most people, you've not given too much thought to the meaning and purpose of your life; or maybe, in the worst-case scenario, you feel that it's meaningless or even that a punishment. Alternatively, you may have put yourself under a lot of pressure by constantly searching for meaning; if that's the case, then, consciously or unconsciously, you've been looking for your purpose or for the thing that would give meaning to everything you've experienced.

I'd sensed very early on that everything in life has a deeper meaning, so I'd embarked on a quest to find *my* meaning. I was constantly looking for my path and I questioned everything I did. *Is what I'm doing now really my life's purpose? Is this the reason I've been put on this Earth, with this family and in this body? What's my soul's calling, my mission, and how can I live it?*

I wasted a lot of time pondering the answers to these questions, and because I couldn't find answers that *felt* right, I always had the sense I was doing the wrong thing. And since I'd been living such an unconscious life, I was subject to intense doubt and self-judgment. But the worst thing was the pressure I put on myself. During my near-death experience, I looked back on my life and all the sad decisions I'd made, and naturally those familiar questions arose once more: *What is the meaning of all this? Why have I chosen this life? What did I do wrong?*

My teacher gave me the following answer: 'You've done nothing wrong! It just depends on the perspective from which you look at your life. You, as a human being, assume in your limited imagination that life is about doing or not doing something. You think there's a path, a plan, and a goal that you must reach, but there isn't! You think you can do something right or wrong, but that's not true either. That's not the point. The real purpose of your life is to find out what makes you *you*, and to then express it!'

As soon as we start to make the most
of our abilities, life becomes easy.

Being our 'authentic self' certainly sounds right, but do we really know what it means? It's instilled in us from a young age that self-development is painstakingly hard work, and that it takes a long time, but the opposite is true! As soon as you start to follow your inner joy, passion, and enthusiasm, it becomes easy. Because as soon as we listen to the lightness and joy within us, we notice it more and more.

As soon as we stop letting ourselves be led by the thinker, and instead learn that it's OK to be led by joy, miracles begin to happen. What excites you? What captivates you? What sets your heart on fire? What fulfils you? If you're one of those people who know exactly what they *don't* want, it's about time you found out what you *do* want, because that's where your talents lay hidden.

Key 6: Listen to Your Body

As I've explained, my teacher tried very hard to get me to make friends with my body. Without scolding me or pushing me, he patiently showed me its magic over and over again. Although my father, as a naturopathic doctor, has always approached the body holistically, this way of thinking went completely over my head. I'd always thought it was enough to take reasonable care of my body, to feed it well, to have the occasional medical check-up and, when it felt really worn out, to take a bath or sleep a little longer.

But when I really got to know my body, I was amazed to discover that it was quite indifferent to all of that. My teacher helped me to realize that the body reacts solely to vibrations because it's a field of pure resonance; it reacts to the vibration of the food we eat, to the colors of the clothes we wear, to our thoughts, and especially to how we feel about ourselves. However, if we know nothing about the body's consciousness or the way it reacts to us, we end up with little opportunity to recognize all the miracles it holds. We use it and look after it, but we don't consciously *inhabit* it. My teacher helped me to see my body as a unity of color, vibration, and sound, and I was truly amazed when I consciously entered its universe.

When I learned to really work with my body, to speak its language, everything changed. But how does the body speak to us? Well, we know that it signals problems through pain or illness, but it has another way of communicating with us that's more constant and which we can learn to understand much sooner. Our *feelings* are the body's true language, and they're something we know inside out.

Remember the sparkly gold dots I told you about, which live in every one of the 80 trillion cells in your body? They're directly connected to the Source, and they react to you – if you send them love, they'll be delighted to send your own love back to you, twofold. Your body speaks to you through the language of feelings, and you communicate with it most easily through your emotional level.

When I began to figure out how I could give my new life a different direction, my body helped me by showing me what worked for me and what didn't. If something felt light and pleasant, I knew I was on the right track. If I noticed any unpleasant sensations or felt heavy, I knew I was headed back to my old life.

Your body is the part of you that meets other people, that resonates with them. You use its eyes to see, its ears to hear, and its mouth to speak your words so that they can be heard by other ears. You use its hands to touch people and animals with your frequency. Everything that you as a human being want to give to other people and experience for yourself is done through your physical body and your consciousness.

Fulfilment isn't possible outside
of your body; fulfilment cannot be
experienced without your body.

The greatest love affair you should ever have is with your own body. It's been made especially for you – it's your direct line to the Source because it's connected to it through your cells.

It carries everything you need for your journey onward, and much, much more. Before you continue reading, it might be a good idea to flick back to Chapter 10 and reread it. The golden dots of light in your cells are your amazing body's resonance field and you can make them vibrate and dance at any time – and equally they can do the same for you.

Key 7: Know That Nothing Exists Outside of You

Our perception that we're isolated, separate individuals is the greatest illusion and the greatest obstacle of all because in truth, *everything* is interconnected. You are an inseparable part of God, Creation, or whatever you want to call your connection to the Source. It's constantly acting through you and expressing itself through you. Just as breathing is something that you do without thinking, in the same way, you're inseparably connected to everything.

The reason we're unable to perceive this miracle is because we're trapped inside the cocoon I talked about earlier (see Chapters 7, 12, and 16). That's why we look for fulfilment, love, and our soul externally. We look outside ourselves and pray to God; we hope that someone else will love us unconditionally because we don't feel that love within us; and we seek support and direction outside ourselves. We're conditioned to do this, and no one's ever taught us that it's all a fallacy. When I work with people, I see their emptiness, their inner fight with themselves, and I feel their despair. They believe they've lost themselves; they've repressed their feelings and they feel that they're powerless. But it's not true.

You already have all that you need, and when you stop looking for it on the outside, you'll realize that everything you've been longing for already exists within you. Trust me, I know what I'm talking about – I'm living proof of it. I didn't want to return to my body because I thought in doing so, I'd lose all the wonderful things I'd seen in the spiritual realm. But the opposite was true. Today, I'm able to experience all of that and more, *in* my body. Everything is connected to everything else through you.

For me, there are no longer two separate worlds – the spiritual and the material – and I don't feel disconnected or empty inside. I'm connected to the vibration of my nameless teacher just as I'm connected to everything else that I experienced. I dance between the two worlds, and I feel equally at home in both. But perhaps most importantly of all, I've learned to love my life.

The golden key for you is to see your
soul. You're inseparably connected to
its limitless field of consciousness.

Your soul knows everything about you, and it knows your path. What if you stopped looking for it on the outside, and instead consciously drew it from within? What if you allowed yourself to open the doors you've closed and let your soul, your spiritual guides, and God in? What if you gave yourself the love you crave? I'd like to remind you that in the field of infinite possibilities, everything you think is possible is available to you, and what you attract into your life is within your control. You are *not* separate.

Give it a try and allow yourself to be surprised. Imagine drawing everything that's good, everything you need, into yourself like a magnet. With each in breath, draw what you thought you'd lost back into yourself. If you're afraid of life, try to consciously absorb all the wonderful qualities of planet Earth – its stability, wisdom, and infinite creativity. Feel what changes inside you, and then breathe your soul into your body. Feel *yourself*.

Key 8: Love Yourself

Humanity's a funny thing if you look at it from a 'big picture' perspective. We already have everything, and I mean *everything*, within us that we need to live a fulfilling life. We come into the world possessing this knowledge, but then as we learn to adapt to society and other people, and begin to follow role models instead of our gut instinct, we're pulled away from ourselves.

Many people struggle to express the vibration from which we all emerged, the vibration that carries us and is anchored in every cell in the body. And most people struggle to love themselves. They think that to practice self-love they need to *do* something. They think they must earn it or give something – to themselves or to others. They believe they must perform or behave in a certain way to be deemed worthy of love. But none of that is true. You don't have to do anything. No matter what has been or what will be, and no matter what other people have taught you.

You're here on Earth to learn about unconditional love and you're still learning – we all are – so don't put pressure on yourself. It would serve you well to be an attentive student who's eager to study hard; after all, love is the most important and beautiful subject you can study at the School of Life. Maybe you can begin by treating yourself with a little more love and kindness. Cut yourself some slack and acknowledge all the wonderful qualities you possess.

Perhaps you're more used to feeling love for other people or seeking love from others, but this is all about *you*. To develop unconditional self-love, you must acknowledge yourself fully and completely, exactly as you are right now – and know that you're *perfect* just the way you are, and you always have been. The truth is, you've done nothing wrong and there's nothing to blame yourself for. From your soul's point of view, there's nothing that makes you less worthy and there's no reason why you should feel small or dependent. There's nothing to feel guilty about, nothing to repent for, and no one to judge you – except yourself.

You don't have to perform a certain service to earn love, nor do you have to change anything about yourself to be worthy of it. Love is *fully* available to you, no matter how much you're convinced that it's not. Try to stop looking outside yourself for love and start looking inward and loving yourself. The more you learn to value and love yourself, the more you'll understand that you aren't separate, broken, or wrong. You'll realize that it's up to you whether you want to change something, keep it, or leave it. The result is a feeling of deep inner peace that fulfils you and makes you smile.

Remember that you're here to
experience and learn all about love
because that's your true nature.

As soon as you start to love yourself, you come into your power. You don't owe anything to anyone, and you don't have to put up with anything that you don't want to. You learn that you can change everything whenever you choose to or accept things as they are. As soon as you start to love yourself, you learn to stop giving your power to others and to trust your own gut instinct. You take responsibility for yourself, but not for the things that have nothing to do with you. You stop following other people's paths and start to recognize your own – and that is truly glorious.

You learn to let yourself be guided by your joy, your intuition, and your body, which allows you to find the ease within yourself that's your true nature. You feel a deep sense of peace because you've stopped bending over backward to please other people, conforming, and submitting. And you start to *follow* your own path. Step by step. In whatever direction you choose.

CHAPTER 19

You Are a Miracle

If I could give you one thing in life, it would be the ability to see yourself through the eyes of your True Self, even for just a moment – for you to see yourself as the miracle that you really are. But I know that this opportunity *will* come for you. Sooner or later, you'll acknowledge that you're complete and perfect, and you'll stand in awe of everything that makes you *you*.

Just as I did, one day you'll look back on your life, and I truly hope that this will be fulfilling for you. Please, don't forget that no matter where you are in life right now, you have the choice to change everything, if you want to. That's exactly what I did. After returning to this life for a second time, I didn't hesitate to rid myself of anything that had come before and to let my True Self take the reins. Even though at the beginning I didn't know what it would mean for me or where it would take me, it was clear that I couldn't possibly resume the unconscious life I'd had before the fire.

Far too often, we humans live our lives in a continual state of avoidance. We try to avoid the pain that life or, more specifically, the world around us, reflects back at us. We act from a place of lack and are therefore always busy doing, achieving, or proving something. We believe every word the thinker in us has to say and as a result we feel small and powerless.

During my experience, my avoidance strategies turned into complete surrender. I learned to accept my fears, doubts, and insecurities and saw them for the illusions they were. Any preconceived notions I had about life disappeared when I learned to deprive my mind of the security of its thoughts. I let go of all that I thought I knew about karma, God, or the nature of my body, and of course that was incredibly unsettling for my mind. I became aware that every belief I held, no matter how logical it sounded, was only an opinion and it didn't correspond with my reality.

Discover Your Personal Truth

When you've had an experience like mine, it's pretty easy to give up your belief in God, but the thing is, you then tend to sell your own truth to other people as the ultimate truth or try to teach them what you've learned. And in doing so, you're simply adopting a new belief and imposing your newly acquired knowledge onto them. You're just replacing your old viewpoint with a new one and trying to adapt it to your own little world.

*There is no truth except that which
you alone experience as truth.*

I'm immersed in my own personal truth. It's a truth so multidimensional and so multifaceted that I can only describe it as a limitless, all-embracing miracle. It expresses itself differently for everyone, and it's *my* truth. It's up to you to discover *your* truth and to see the miracles in your reality. You are individual, unique, and complete – and that's an irrefutable fact, no matter what the thinker in you has to say about it.

I've learned that anything – and I mean *anything* – is possible and it's completely up to me which miracles I want to experience in my life. Now, more than a decade after the accident, I still pay very conscious attention to the hidden beliefs that shape my life and I work to unpick them as soon as I become aware of them.

I know now that I'm not here in this body to achieve anything, prove anything, or explain anything. I'm not here to make the world a better place or to make a difference. Nobody is here to do that. I'm here to recognize myself for what I really am. I'm here to break the boundaries of my lower, unconscious self and to experience the space beyond that within myself. I'm here in this body to express all the joy and ease of living that makes my heart feel like it's about to explode. I can change the world around me by simply expressing myself.

Instead of looking for something on the outside to fulfil me on the inside, my life now reflects my inner fulfilment. We're all pure, resonating bodies, which means that we all resonate with each other through our vibrational fields, and life is simply the mirror that reflects this back at us. Just as my old life reflected my fears and my limiting beliefs back at me, it now mirrors the infinite possibilities at my disposal.

Embodying Love

Nothing in my life today has anything to do with the woman I used to be – except for her name, perhaps. But even this has now lost all meaning because I'm so much more than a name. From my higher level of consciousness, I'm neither a woman nor a person of a specific age; I'm not my body or my thoughts.

Truth be told, I'm not the words I write for you either, and nothing I do matters. I'm pure vibration; I'm constantly expressing myself on all levels via everything I choose to focus my awareness on. Everything I used to think was important, unchangeable, and real has turned out to be false. Time as I once knew it has lost all meaning, and even the space I move in, whether in my body, my house, or the world itself, merges into one in an unlimited and fluid way.

My mind has largely said goodbye to its old thought patterns and is mostly still and at peace with itself. This awareness doesn't give meaning to anything except the appreciation and recognition I give to my body and to life itself. If we live in recognition and appreciation, we automatically embody love – love for ourselves, for life, and for other people. Anything else is no longer possible.

Today, my life feels very similar to how it did when my body was in a coma. The greatest gift for me is that I now get to experience this miracle from inside my body. I feel eternally grateful to my teacher for his perseverance. If he hadn't brought me back to my body, I guarantee I wouldn't be here today. If he hadn't done all that he possibly could to change my narrow and limited view of my life and my body, I wouldn't have been able to have all these experiences that I hope will never stop.

Going Deeper

Here's another golden key to life: Knowledge alone changes nothing; knowledge alone doesn't enable us to grow – it's simply food for the mind. Just hearing, reading, or understanding something doesn't help us on our journey, but if we learn something important and then allow ourselves to *experience* it, everything changes.

I could tell you so many things about all the miracles that life may have in store for you, but if you've read my words without really absorbing them then this book was probably nothing more than an interesting read to you. However, if you're willing to let my words flow a little deeper, they'll resonate with your vibrational signature.

I'd like to invite you to undertake a little experiment now so you can experience this for yourself. You can think of it as a mind game in which you, too, have full access to the Source and can express your True Self.

Meditation: Your Journey to the Source

Imagine that everything you've read in this book about my journey to eternity is now *your* journey to eternity. Are you ready? Let's go...

An incredible, nameless teacher visits you while your body is asleep. He suddenly appears at your bedside and invites you to accompany him on a very special journey. Just let your body continue to sleep as you enter your teacher's infinite, brightly shining energy field. Allow him to take you in his arms; imagine how good this feels and how quickly you relax.

Imagine him gently pulling you out of the room where your body lies sleeping, and that with each breath, you begin to feel lighter and lighter. In your teacher's arms, everything that's ever felt heavy and tight in your life simply falls away from you and it continues to do so the more you let yourself be absorbed by his wonderful energy. All your worries disappear, and your thoughts and feelings lose all meaning. Nothing matters except your teacher carrying you further and further into an unconditional state of lightness and ease. Space and time don't matter; all that matters is that you can continue to expand.

You notice that, at the same time as you're expanding, you can connect with everything around you. Everything seems to happen as if by magic because your teacher is trying to make you aware of something vitally important. He wants to show you that you are much, much more than you've ever thought possible. The reality you are so magically immersed in now is unconditional and it can only be controlled by your own consciousness.

Now your teacher wants you to focus on experiencing your True Self. You'll probably find yourself quickly expanding, further and further, and slipping into a state that opens your consciousness. You're now in the field of infinite possibilities, and wherever you want to go, all it takes is a single thought to get you there. Everything you observe here consists of an infinite number of colors, frequencies, vibrations, and qualities – all of which resonate and are interwoven in an incredibly intricate way – and you are one magnificent part of it. You realize that everything in you and around you is high-vibration, and yet you still have a clear sense of self.

Suddenly, you understand what connects you to everything around you: consciousness. No matter where you look, no matter where you want to go, everything that surrounds you is as self-aware as you are. You know that you're a part of Creation and you know how you like to express yourself.

From your own limitlessness consciousness, you once sent a part of your wonderful being to Earth and into a human body in order to experience duality and to understand space and time. This part of you is currently on a journey of forgetting because they no longer know that they're fully connected to you and to the Source.

This part of you is immersed in a world of contradictions; a thinking mind, or ego, enveloped their radiant field of light at an early age, giving them a sense of security and direction in their new world, all so that they could adapt to being human. Over the course of their life, it developed into a thick cocoon that made them forget where they'd come from.

You yourself, of course, always know where this part of you is on their adventurous journey and you've always been there to love and support them along the way. You were a part of all their experiences because you're a part of them and they're a part of you. Perhaps you'd like to focus on this part of yourself? Would you like to consciously take the cocoon that holds this little human being into your hands? The cocoon contains a world of contradictions, feelings, and thoughts that this person you are so deeply connected to thinks is real.

This is the perfect time to help that part of you remember your True Self. You could help them wake up from their dream, so that they can recognize as illusions the limitations they think are their reality. For this little person in their cocoon has simply forgotten that they were once a magnificent part of something much greater and that they're connected to the infinite possibilities of the Source.

Take this opportunity to gently and lovingly remind them of this. Perhaps you might send them all the love and appreciation you feel for them so they can sense your presence. You could tell them that most of what they're convinced is their reality isn't true. You could tell them that they've never done anything wrong and that there's nothing wrong with them. You could tell them that there's nothing to feel guilty about and nothing to atone for. You could tell them that there's no one to assess or judge them, and that you've never, ever forgotten them.

I'm sure they're listening attentively to your words. I'm sure your words sound like the divine cosmic choir whose vibration they've stored in every one of their cells. Tell this part of you how much you love them and how proud they should be for having embarked on such an adventurous journey. Remind them of their true home and tell them that they can expand their cocoon all by themselves and remember everything when they realize that they were never separate from the Source. They are still pure, unconditional love. They never have been and never will be anything other than love.

Now pour into the cocoon everything that this part of you needs – the love they can't find within themselves, the connection they so long for, and the appreciation you feel for them. If you wish, you can change your perspective and take on the role of the person inside the cocoon, so you can feel how much your True Self surrounds you and even permeates you. So you can feel the unconditional love and appreciation your True Self has for you. Embrace it! Breathe all these qualities deep into your body and let yourself be fully immersed.

That's who you really are. You're inside and outside at the same time. You're inside your cocoon but also outside it because separation is only an illusion. You're everything and you're also connected to everything. You always have been, and you always will be. You are your True Self, and at the same time you're also the person experiencing life in your body. You're infinite and connected to everything, even if you'd forgotten that until now.

You are the Source that constantly expresses itself through you. Nothing else is possible. Your life's purpose is to realize that and to experience it. Your purpose is to find yourself, and to know that you are much, much more than the limiting beliefs you hold about yourself.

You're a miracle in a human body because you have a consciousness that you can expand infinitely. With your consciousness, you can take on any point of view you wish. You can use your focus to control and change your reality – anytime you like. You're both inside and outside, and perhaps you've even realized that inside and outside don't even exist. Everything is connected to everything else through you. You've just forgotten.

This is what truly loving yourself means:

◊   Self-love has nothing to do with positive affirmations or mantras.

◊   Self-love is much more than a *word*.

◊   Self-love is much more than a *feeling*.

◊   Self-love is *knowing* how wonderful you are.

◊   Self-love is *acknowledging* yourself.

◊   Self-love is *valuing* yourself.

◊   Self-love is *self-fulfilment*.

Please remember that nothing exists outside of you.

Making Peace with Ourselves

One of the beautiful things I took away from my near-death experience is the understanding that life can be really *easy* if you let it. Life becomes a miracle when we finally stop expecting our wishes to be granted by something or someone outside ourselves. As soon as we start to make peace with ourselves and acknowledge that *we* are the main focus of our lives, things become much easier.

> *Life is an incredible gift! If we used*
> *even a fraction of the opportunities*
> *that are presented to us, we'd be among*
> *the world's most fulfilled people.*

What feels good to you? What brings you joy? What do you believe in? What are you convinced of? As I asked myself these questions repeatedly, I realized that I'd categorized almost everything into one of two camps: right or wrong. The world is full of rules that someone made for themselves at some point, rules that became established and are now widely considered unbreakable. If I believe that things like sin or guilt exist, then of course I'll be proven right. Because if I put some higher power on a pedestal, I'll make myself feel small and powerless, and I'll always be terrified of doing something wrong.

But is what we believe *really* true? Wasn't it once widely believed that the Earth is flat? Is someone who believes in many gods or someone who rejects the very idea of God worth less than a Christian? Is it really true that the body will become frail in old age or that we don't get to decide when we die? Is it really true that we're stuck in a cycle of karma, or is this maybe just another reason to continue feeling like a victim of circumstance? Are the beliefs we live by really true, or do we just continue to adopt old, traditional ideas without ever questioning them?

Today, I no longer follow traditional ideas or to-do lists, and I certainly don't conform to specific methods or guidelines. Instead, I always live in the moment and in a way that feels right for me at the time. For me, the miracle of life is its diversity and changeability, and I'm constantly changing with it.

You Are a Vibration

I hope with all my heart that you remember the lightness, ease, and love that dwell within you. I hope with all my heart that you recognize yourself as the divine being that you always have been and always will be. You are a miracle, the body you inhabit is a miracle, and the world around you is a miracle. You're alive in this moment, living and breathing as you read these words. Notice yourself as you exhale and wait eagerly for what follows next. If you open your consciousness to opportunity, life can be a never-ending miracle. Perhaps you can hear the soft ticking of a clock in the background, or another sound that your ears pick up.

You inhale, a little deeper than before. Your lungs look a bit like wings – could they be those of a butterfly or even an angel?

You exhale, more softly this time. Your heart is pumping blood through your veins, your cells are dividing, and maybe you can even feel the steady vibration of the dancing gold dots within them.

You inhale again, a little more consciously than before. *What's she getting at?* you wonder, as your eyes follow the words on the page. You exhale. You're present in the moment. Can you feel it? You're attentive, you're present, reading the words on this page, but you're also aware of your body.

Every single moment is unique, and one after the other, together these moments make up our lives. We live through countless meaningful moments, but mostly without really noticing them, and meanwhile they're breathing, flowing, and renewing themselves within us. You are a miracle, and you have the power to focus your consciousness and attention on this miracle. Your vibration flows and changes without interruption.

You are no longer the same person you were a few moments ago; you're a brand-new you. And in a few moments, there will be yet another new you, because you are vibration. Then, in a few minutes, it won't matter who you are because by then you'll be an even newer you. Your body will vibrate differently to how it does now, and you'll focus on something else. You may make a decision that will overwrite everything that's gone before, or you may even begin to fall in love with yourself. Who knows?

Here's Your Wake-Up Call, My Beloved

You are *free*.
Free to do whatever brings you joy and makes your heart sing.
Make a decision for yourself and say *yes* to yourself.

You are *free*.
Free to let go of everything that holds you back because you're not obliged to do anything except be yourself. Choose to be free! You already are.

You are *free*.
Free to find your own truth, make your own decisions, and act on them. Decide to take responsibility for your life and choose how you want to live.

You are *free*.
Free to focus on the ease that your body and your feelings are communicating to you. Decide to live and express your truth from now on. You're worth it.

You are *free*.
Free to live your life *for* yourself from now on, instead of *against* yourself. Lay down your weapons and make peace.

Everything else will arrive of its own accord.

You and Me

The miracles I've experienced as multidimensional consciousness have become a physical reality for me, and today I'm at my happiest when I'm supporting others on the path to finding their True Self. I love to share my experiences in seminars and workshops, so I can witness the participants' transformations live. Nothing is more fulfilling to me than this because I can see myself in each and every one of those people.

We've now reached the end of our journey together, but it's also only the beginning – for you and for me. You know, life very often presents us with special gifts and it's up to us whether we accept or reject them. The same goes for this book, and I'm delighted that I was able to write it for you. *You* are a gift, too. You're a miracle, and you can be anything your heart desires. Please, never forget that!

I hope from the bottom of my heart that this book has sown some seeds in you that will sprout and flower and bear you the most wonderful fruits. I hope it's resonated with you and perhaps even had the power to help you make some valuable changes in your life.

You can find more information about me and subscribe to my newsletter on my website: www.anke-evertz.de. I'll keep you posted on upcoming offers and send you a fresh source of inspiration from time to time to help you break free from your cocoon and remember!

With love and admiration for you and your Creation,

Anke

Photo by Sladjana Radujkovic

About the Author

Anke Evertz likes to say she is a person with two lives – one before her death and one after. In September 2009, Anke went through an extraordinary, all-encompassing near-death experience. Her life changed fundamentally after this nine-day spiritual experience.

Since then, she has been sharing her insights with thousands of people in courses, seminars and on TV. Today she is a sought-after speaker at many events and passes on her wisdom in an authentic and warm manner to remind people of their true nature.

You can find many interviews about Anke and her story on YouTube and on her website.

www.anke-evertz.de

HAY HOUSE
Online Video Courses

Your journey to a better life starts with figuring out which path is best for you. Hay House Online Courses provide guidance in mental and physical health, personal finance, telling your unique story, and so much more!

CONNECT WITH
HAY HOUSE
ONLINE

Find out all about our latest books & card decks • Be the first to know about exclusive discounts • Interact with our authors in live broadcasts • Celebrate the cycle of the seasons with us • Watch free videos from your favourite authors • Connect with like-minded souls

'*The gateways to wisdom and knowledge are always open.*'

Louise Hay